M000106411

ESTATE PLANNING FOR DOMESTIC PARTNERS

The Legal Secrets You Need to Know
to Protect Your Partner and Your Future

Jeffrey G. Marsocci, Esq.

Domestic Partner Publishing, LLC

Note regarding legal counsel

As with any product, it is important to be clear about its intended purpose and use to avoid any misunderstandings. Specifically with writings about legal issues, it is noted that these materials are not a substitute for competent legal counsel. The contents of this book are instead written to provide information about common estate planning problems faced by domestic partners, and it is designed for general educational purposes only. The contents of this book are not to be construed as legal advice, and no attorney-client privilege exists between the reader and the author and/or publisher. In addition, laws change frequently, and therefore you also are urged to speak with an attorney about changes in the law that may affect you.

Circular 230 Disclosure: To ensure compliance with requirements imposed by the Internal Revenue Service, unless specifically indicated otherwise, any tax advice contained in this communication (including any accompanying literature) was not intended or written to be used, and cannot be used, for the purpose of avoiding tax-related penalties or promoting, marketing, or recommending to another party any tax-related matter addressed herein. For specific legal advice, you are urged to contact an attorney in your state or jurisdiction.

About the Author

Jeffrey G. Marsocci was born in Fort Worth, Texas, and raised in Lincoln, Rhode Island, where he graduated from Mount Saint Charles Academy High School. He received his Bachelor's degree in Business from Hofstra University, and two years later earned his law degree from the same university.

In 2004, he received a Certificate Degree in Non-Profit Management from Duke University, and has earned his Legal Master of Estate Preservation designation from the *Abts Institute for Estate Preservation*. Jeff also serves as a member of the Legal Council for The Estate Plan, a nationally recognized estate preservation company headed by Henry Abts, trust guru and author of *The Living Trust*.

Jeff has led his own firm in Raleigh, North Carolina, since 1996, focusing on the areas of Wills, Trusts and Life & Estate Planning with a concentration in assisting domestic partners and other unmarried couples. He is also a founding member of The National Institute for Domestic Partner Estate Planning, and he frequently participates in programs to educate attorneys, financial advisors and accountants on estate planning issues.

Jeff and his wife Kathleen are active Kiwanis members, working with the college-based service organization Circle K throughout North Carolina and South Carolina. Jeff and Kathy also each received the President's Call to Service Award for performing more than 4,000 hours of service during their lifetimes.

To receive a free gift worth $39.97, please go to
www.estateplanningfordomesticpartners.com/gift

This book is dedicated to my father Gerald and my grandfathers Rudy and Jerry who taught me to stand up for what is right, and to my mother Betsy and grandmothers Mary and Jane who taught me to put other people first.

TABLE OF CONTENTS

To receive a free gift worth $39.97, please go to
www.estateplanningfordomesticpartners.com/gift

To receive a free gift worth $39.97, please go to
www.estateplanningfordomesticpartners.com/gift

Introduction

I would like to welcome you and thank you for picking up this book. Chances are if you are reading this, you are part of a domestic partnership, you care about someone who is in a domestic partnership, or you are a professional who wishes to help domestic partners with their life and estate planning. In all cases, you have come to the right place.

It is clear there are very few places in the United States that offer protection for unmarried couples, particularly same-gender partners. As this book is being written, there are still efforts in Congress to make it unconstitutional for states to recognize same-gender marriages and offer legal protection to partners who have been together for decades yet are routinely denied the right to make emergency medical decisions for each other. When a partner falls ill, estranged family members have the right to step in, kick out the other partner, and take charge of the money the couple worked together to accumulate. Laws are constantly being proposed to openly discriminate against gay couples, and the fight for equality will continue for years to come.

Until then, the rights not given to domestic partners can be seized through documents and techniques that are available to every individual. The question becomes "Who can help us achieve as many equal rights as possible?"

There are some professionals who can help. But domestic partner life and estate planning is one of the most difficult areas of law to understand, mainly because there is no independent body of law focused on it. Because there are no "domestic partner laws" in most jurisdictions, few professionals are willing to venture into the field in a meaningful way. Many who do, try to be a "one-stop-shop" for all areas related to domestic partnerships. They often fail to address some of the nuances of estate planning because they are in court handling adoptions or discrimination cases. Without many professionals using their knowledge and abilities to develop the field of domestic partner life and estate planning, finding a competent attorney, financial advisor or accountant

To receive a free gift worth $39.97, please go to
www.estateplanningfordomesticpartners.com/gift

1

remains a hit-or-miss proposition. It is not really the fault of the individual professionals—after all, if there are no large treatises, guidelines or other general materials to help them help their domestic partner estate planning clients, there is little they can do.

However, this is small comfort to domestic partners when they have to protect themselves. This does not even begin to address the fact that there are professionals who have a decent knowledge of domestic partner solutions but will refuse to openly help because it may drive off other clients.

On the opposite side, there are professionals who offer their services, but in their attempts to apply solutions better suited to married couples, may do more harm than good. The most common example are real estate attorneys who offer to take the $300,000 home of one partner and make it "joint property with a right of survivorship" with the other partner so that the home is owned jointly. While this sounds like a good idea, what actually happened is the partner with the home just gave his or her partner a $150,000 gift which is a taxable transaction and may have severe gift tax consequences.

Now that I have warned you about professionals who may not know exactly what they are doing, I would like to warn you about the biggest document threat out there—office supply store legal kits and the do-it-yourselfers who buy them. While no one understands your situation better than you, you cannot be an expert on everything. That is why professionals like doctors, accountants and attorneys go through years of training and have to be certified by professional boards before they are allowed to practice their trade.

In my observation, the biggest and most costly mistakes are made not by attorneys but by individuals who create their own legal documents. Whenever there is an estate that is "just a complete mess" because there are contradictory clauses, phrases used inaccurately, and sentences with no recognizable legal meaning, the estate invariably has been written by someone with no legal background. When the laws are already stacked against you and your partner, creating the right life and estate plan is not something you want to attempt by yourself, because by the time you discover the errors, it may be too late to fix them.

In reading up on life and estate planning, I have found there are relatively few books devoted to helping domestic partners, and those that do address issues such as powers of attorney and wills at a very basic level. Rarely do non-professional books even mention the "gift tax," which is the single biggest obstacle in domestic partners combining their property outright. Rarely will the texts mention the benefits of using a revocable living trust rather than will, and even more rare will a book address the issues involved in creating a joint revocable living trust. Thus far, I have not seen any books that discuss domestic partners seizing estate tax breaks, such as those enjoyed by married couples.

Without the law, without experienced professionals, and without literature that not only covers the basics but also details advanced planning techniques, domestic partners are left to fend for themselves. This book is meant to address the last two items so domestic partners can find the right people to help them. (We'll leave changes in the law to the politicians and The People.) By using this book and acting upon what you read, you will hopefully be able to find a professional in your jurisdiction that can help you achieve your goals.

In order to help domestic partners find people to help them, I have joined with a few experienced professionals to create an institute devoted to educating and certifying people to help domestic partners. The National Institute for Domestic Partner Estate Planning provides training and certification to these professionals to ensure they are familiar with the goals and obstacles unique to domestic partner planning. An attorney is designated by the Institute as a Legal Master of Partner Planning (LMPP), and a financial advisor or certified public accountant is designated a Master of Partner Planning (MPP).

In order to receive these designations, individuals have to be in good standing with their professional boards, current on their licenses, and complete four days of intense estate planning instruction with emphasis on domestic partner planning concepts and theories. They must also pass two exams—one related to general estate planning concepts and the other specifically on domestic partner planning issues. Additionally, they receive periodic information and instruction from the Institute and must pass an exam every two years to maintain certification. While domestic partners have to feel comfortable with the professionals they work with and always should make their own independent review of credentials, professionals certified by the National Institute for Domestic Partner Estate Planning are a good place to start.

These professionals are also encouraged to work with a professional education and document production company called The Estate Plan. Based in Reno, Nevada, The Estate Plan works with financial advisors, accountants and attorneys to create life and estate planning documents for all individuals and couples to realize their goals. They have a nationwide network of professionals who can help, and I am honored to be affiliated with their efforts. I have lectured several times on domestic partner planning at their annual Advanced Institute, and I am available to all of their advisors as a resource in providing the knowledge and skill.

Because of The Estate Plan's excellent documents and their willingness to help preserve the estates of all people, I refer to their documents frequently herein as a sort of national standard for estate planning. In addition, The Estate Plan now has the Partner AB-SECURE™ Revocable Living Trust created by my office, so it can now be utilized by experienced professional nationwide. But, as with any book on legal and tax matters, the only actual legal advice I will give is to contact an attorney in your jurisdiction with specific estate planning questions for your situation.

This book is divided into three main sections--the basics are covered in chapters one through five, revocable living trusts are covered in chapters seven through ten, and more advanced techniques are covered in chapters eleven through fifteen. I seriously debated having a separate section on "Problems Faced by Domestic Partners," but decided that as a reader of this book, you probably understand the problems better than I could ever explain it. Therefore, examples of problems are discussed along with solutions throughout the book and not as a separate section.

To receive a free gift worth $39.97, please go to
www.estateplanningfordomesticpartners.com/gift

In addition to the information in this book, there are also a number of resources and free reports referenced in these pages, and more information is being added all of the time. For a current list of audio programs and resources, please go to www.theestategeek.com.

With this said, please read on and act upon what you learn to obtain legal advice for your estate planning. All of this information amounts to nothing but words on paper if you do not take action. Again, thank you for reading and taking control of a better, more protected life for domestic partners.

SECTION I:
THE BASICS

In Section I, you will find an overview of the contents in this book, along with information on basic life planning documents related to healthcare and finances. These are the critical documents both partners should not be without, even if they do not plan to take any further steps in planning their estates together. By reading through and understanding this section, you will see that while domestic partners are not given many rights under the law, there are steps that can be taken to empower each other and gain many rights married couples take for granted.

Chapter One:
Overview

Domestic partners are at a distinct legal disadvantage compared to married couples. Hundreds of years of legal precedence, statutes and cases have been compiled, automatically giving couples special rights and privileges upon marriage. Until same-gender couples are legally allowed to marry, they will never gain the advantages and rights marriage confers. In this chapter, we will address some of the basic problems domestic partners face and pair them with solutions, which will be covered later in the book.

Before getting too deeply into solutions, it is probably best to review some common misconceptions in domestic partner planning. Far too often, people with a little bit of knowledge believe they know everything, yet this can lead to more harm than good. Using wills, joint property, and beneficiary designations, and all of their drawbacks, will be discussed in Chapter Two.

One of the most basic rights given to spouses and denied to domestic partners is the ability to make medical decisions for the other. If a married person becomes too sick to make informed medical decisions, or is unable to communicate his or her wishes, the spouse can step in to make those decisions for them. In most states, the closest living relative (sometimes known as the "next of kin") automatically becomes the person to make medical decisions, and the spouse is considered to be the closest relative, usually followed by the children.

Even though individual states have their own laws that define who are the closest living relatives to make these medical decisions, legal adults in all states can opt out of using the statute and instead create a healthcare power of attorney document to assign people to make those decisions for them. Now they can choose relatives and/or non-relatives to make medical decisions for them if they can't. Healthcare powers of attorney are covered in more detail in Chapter Three.

Amidst all of the assigning of powers in domestic partnerships, we should not lose focus of one of the most contentious and personal issues out there—whether or not to discontinue life support and artificial nutrition and hydration. If a doctor determines there is no hope of recovery under your state's medical standards, do you want to be kept alive on machines and feeding tubes?

Unless you take steps to assign another person, this decision also falls upon your closest living relative. If you have a properly drafted healthcare power of attorney, it typically permits your healthcare agent to make those decisions. However, many people do not want to place that burden on anyone. That is what a living will is for. Most states allow you to make your own decision in these areas ahead of time and put them into a legal document so once a doctor determines your diagnosis, there is no further decision needed by anyone else. You have already made your decision in writing. Living Wills and Nomination of Conservator documents will also be covered in more detail in Chapter Three.

If someone is unable to make his or her own healthcare decisions, it is also very likely the individual will also be unable to handle his or her own finances. In this case, a spouse is usually given wide latitude to manage finances for the incapacitated spouse without many questions or restrictions. While there are some exceptions to these broad spousal powers, they are few, especially when compared to the non-existent powers domestic partners have.

If an unmarried person, whether in a domestic partnership or not, becomes unable to handle his or her own finances, then the individual states each have a process to appoint someone to handle these matters. Unfortunately, many of these statutes still favor relatives over others, regardless of their qualifications, and there is usually a legal proceeding to declare the person incompetent. Aside from being an intrusive and humiliating experience, it can be expensive to institute and costly to administer. Some commentators have termed this process "living probate," and they have done so accurately.

Essentially, a court proceeding is initiated where evidence is presented about the person to be determined incompetent. The court will typically assign a guardian to look out for his or her rights. The individual petitioning the court to declare the person incompetent will present doctor's reports, call witnesses to give testimony, and try to prove the person cannot function adequately in caring for his or her own well-being. If the court determines the person should be declared incompetent, then the court may move to the second phase: determining who should be in charge of the incompetent person's financial affairs and how the court will oversee the finances to make sure nothing inappropriate happens.

It sounds like an involved process, which also means an expensive process, and it is. The simple solution is to have a financial power of attorney. All that is required to activate the power of attorney is for a physician to declare the person unable to handle his or her own finances, and the power of attorney agent can take over. The financial power of attorney described in detail in Chapter Four.

That covers the basic documents recommended to help domestic partners. While these are important areas to review -- they must be completed as part of any comprehensive life and estate plan -- they are not the intermediate or even advanced techniques that will be addressed in this book. The main document to help provide domestic partners many of the same rights as married couples will be discussed in Section II: Revocable Living Trusts. However, I would like to explain a plainly absent document most books recommend as part of domestic partner estate planning—the Last Will and Testament.

A will is necessary, but it is not covered as a separate document in this book. Instead, it is our strongest recommendation that domestic partners look into a joint revocable living trust instead, and specifically consider a Partner AB-SECURE™ Revocable Living Trust through a company called The Estate Plan. There is always a last will and testament for each partner that accompanies a revocable living trust, but it is extremely basic. We will discuss revocable living trusts in great detail in Chapter Five, and you will read that all of the "action" occurs in this trust. The wills are basically in place to handle any forgotten items not placed in the trust before or upon death.

Since the most important estate planning features take place within the revocable living trust, the most important person you and your partner need to choose is your successor trustee. Chapter Six is devoted to suggestions and guidelines in choosing an appropriate trustee.

Chapter Seven discusses the domestic partnership property agreement, a critical document that accompanies a revocable living trust, or, in the case of a Partner AB-SECURE™ Trust, is integrated. The largest barriers to domestic partners in combining their property as one family unit are state and federal gift taxes. A domestic partnership property agreement allows partners to combine their property inside a joint trust without violating gift tax rules and incurring a significant tax burden. Gift taxes are explained in more detail in Chapter Nine.

While joint revocable living trusts can help domestic partners attain many of their goals, assets such as checking accounts, insurance policies, residences and land, have to be titled properly in order for the trust to work. This process, called funding the trust, is covered in detail in Chapter Eight.

In Section III, Chapters Ten through Fourteen, we will review advanced tax savings techniques for domestic partners. These will primarily be used to help reduce or eliminate estate taxes for domestic partners, and in some cases exceed the "average" tax breaks enjoyed by married couples. Chapter Ten will introduce the estate tax, including the changes it will be making through the year 2011.

One advanced estate planning technique is the doubling of estate tax credits for domestic partners just as married couples can through something called a credit shelter trust. As of the writing of this book, each individual dying after 2011 is allowed to pass on $1 million in property without paying any federal estate taxes. There is a special technique used prevalently in estate planning for married couples that allows them to pass up to $2 million to the next generation without estate taxes. Domestic partners do not have this option through the same kind of trust, but the "SECURE™" portion of the Partner AB-SECURE™ Trust we developed in conjunction with The Estate Plan can do the same thing. This is covered in more detail in Chapter Eleven.

Depending on the estate tax and life insurance situation for a domestic partnership, there may be some extensive taxes. While many life insurance salespeople are quick to tell you the beneficiaries do not pay any taxes on life insurance proceeds, they are not so quick to disclose that life insurance proceeds are considered part of your taxable estate. This leads to the widespread misconception that life insurance is completely tax-free for everyone.

While life insurance can considerably increase the value of a person's taxable estate, there is a simple way to take the proceeds out of the taxable estate through an irrevocable life insurance trust (often called an "ILIT" for short). By creating an ILIT, assigning independent trustees, and permanently placing the life insurance policy in the ILIT, these proceeds can avoid being taxed as part of an estate. Using an ILIT will be covered in Chapter Twelve.

If asset equalization is especially important for domestic partners, steps can also be taken to transfer more each year from one partner to another while lowering their overall taxable estates. By using corporations in the right way, domestic partners can equalize their assets, give some assets corporate protection, and even gain estate tax deductions, all while maintaining equal control over the partnership. The correct use of corporations is reviewed in Chapter Thirteen.

As often happens in life, people may not come to relationships with the same amount of assets. Once they have committed themselves to each other, they may wish to equalize their assets for effective tax planning, or simply to have their assets be as equal as their relationship. Married couples are allowed to immediately equalize their assets and own everything together. Domestic partners and other unmarried couples have to equalize their estates gradually in order to avoid triggering the federal gift tax. But it can be done effectively and efficiently, cutting down the number of years it takes to equalize the partners' assets. In Chapter Fourteen, we will review some principles and techniques to plan asset equalization on an annual basis.

As you read this book, I highly recommend you read through Section I, and then carefully read through Section II. The main information most domestic partners need to reach the most typical goals are contained in these sections. While a lot of time was spent breaking down some complex estate tax issues and providing solutions in Section III, it is only applicable to partners whose life insurance proceeds and combined assets exceed $2 million. To determine if your estate requires review for these advanced issues, I have an estate calculation form our firm uses, which as a purchaser of this book, you can receive for free. To download this free Excel format spreadsheet to calculate estate taxes, please go to www.estateplanningfordomesticpartners.com/spreadsheet.

Chapter Two:
Common Misconceptions in
Domestic Partner Estate Planning

Sometimes conventional wisdom is not so wise, and it takes more than advice from a friend to handle things the right way. Unfortunately, a lot of layperson advice gets followed and, in the area of life and estate planning, the problems are not realized until years later. In this chapter, we will review three of the most common life and estate planning mistakes and explain why they are mistakes. (For more information on other planning mistakes frequently made by domestic partners, please download the free report *Five Common Pitfalls in Domestic Partner Estate Planning That Can Cost Thousands of Dollars,* please go to www.domesticpartnerpitfalls.com.)

Specifically, we will look at:

1) Wills

2) Joint Property

3) Beneficiary Designations.

Planning Mistake #1: Using Wills

Probably the most popular document for estate planning is the Last Will and Testament. All adults can spell out their wishes for what happens to their property after they pass on. As long as the format complies with state law and all debts and taxes are taken care of, their property goes to the people chosen. Of course, there are some exceptions in state laws, such as a wife not being able to completely cut out her husband, but by and large property goes to the designated beneficiaries.

A Last Will and Testament can name executors to handle the details of moving your estate through the probate process, nominate guardians to care for minors, and appoint trustees to manage the inheritance for underage beneficiaries. It can also designate beneficiaries, create age and other restrictions and provide specific instructions for handling certain property.

For domestic partners, drafting wills that name each other as beneficiaries may seem like the correct course of action to protect each other. After all, this is what most married couples also do. It is extremely important to note that using a will has some serious drawbacks regardless of your marital situation. First, using a will guarantees your assets go through the probate court before being distributed to your chosen beneficiaries, which means high settlement costs, time delays and a higher possibility of your plans being contested.

Probate is the legal process of transferring title of assets from a deceased person's name to the names of the rightful beneficiaries and heirs. In the most basic terms, probate is a re-titling process. But in order for a court to be assured there is no embezzlement or corruption before transferring those assets, many inventories, appraisals and other tasks have to be completed, documented and reviewed before the court will let things go. It is this process, which was originally designed with good intentions, that causes the drawbacks.

The amount of money spent on the probate process may shock you. There have been numerous studies over the years. While there is considerable variance in the costs associated with probate, I feel comfortable estimating that probate eats up between four and ten percent (4 percent-10 percent) of an estate's assets.

For example, let's say our friends Andy and Barney have not done any life and estate planning except for having wills drawn up. Andy passes away, leaving Barney a condominium that includes furniture and appliances, a stock portfolio, and various other assets totaling $500,000. The rough estimate of probate costs would be between $20,000 and $50,000. There are some law firms that will actually charge a flat rate of five percent of the total value of the estate to handle all matters in settling the estate, so Andy's estate would cost $25,000 to settle.

I can hear probate attorneys mumbling about how that's ridiculous, and how the probate court fees are nowhere nearly that high. They're right. Probate court fees are not that high, but their argument is just like the life insurance salespeople make when they say there are no taxes on life insurance proceeds. The probate court fees are not the issue. What is at issue are all of the attorney fees, appraisals, paperwork and related expenses necessary to complete the probate process. In North Carolina, probate court fees are 40 cents for every $1,000 and are capped at $6,000 in fees. Next time an attorney tells you probate is not that big of a deal and the probate court fees are low, be sure to ask him or her if that includes all of the other filing fees, appraisals and attorney fees as well, and if he or she would put it in writing.

Now, I want to be clear in criticizing some of my fellow attorneys. I have no problem with probate attorneys who take on difficult-to-settle estates. They put a lot time and effort into their work, and it is not their fault the probate court has stringent requirements they have to meet. It is quite probable they deserve every penny of the 4-10 percent they charge. My problem is with estate planning attorneys who tell their clients *during the planning phase* that they don't need to avoid probate for their estates, or that probate is no big deal. These attorneys are either not knowledgeable in avoiding probate, or, much worse, they know exactly what they are doing and are counting on huge legal fees in the future for probating the inexpensive wills they draft now.

It also takes a significant amount of time to probate an estate. Settlement times vary even more greatly than costs, and there are some states with special, more rapid procedures for small estates. However, anywhere between six months and two years is a likely estimate for most estates, and that does not include those estates where the will is contested. Much of this is time is wasted on trips to the courthouse or to the attorney's office, time spent gathering information in order to fill out detailed inventory and report forms, and time spent with your life in a holding pattern while all of the formalities of probate are observed. Even worse, particularly for domestic partner couples, the deceased's accounts may be tied up during probate, leaving the other partner financially handicapped.

Wills are also much more susceptible to challenges than other methods of estate planning, such a revocable living trust. For domestic partners, protecting against challenges from the angry relatives who want to cause trouble may be the primary motivation for even addressing life and estate planning. Attorneys who suggest a Last Will and Testament and nothing more may be unknowingly setting their clients up for a fall.

The reason wills are easier to contest is because a will is formed at one point in time. The most frequent method of contesting a will is claiming the deceased was not "in their right mind" when he or she signed it. All that is needed to cast doubt on the will signing is behavior around the one point in time. Let's say a person saw a psychologist the week before he signed his will. An upset beneficiary may start yelling and screaming "See! He was crazy to cut me out and leave everything to his live-in friend!" The one appointment combined with an emotional plea may be enough to move a judge to at least examine the state of mind of the will signer around the signing date.

This is not the case with a revocable living trust because it is not acted upon only once and not again until death like a will. If someone wanted to prove a person's revocable living trust is invalid because the person was not in her right mind, then someone would have to cast doubt on her actions each and every time she acted with the trust. For example, if Alice's brother doesn't like the fact she is leaving all of her assets to her partner Vera and he wanted to show she was not in her right mind, he would have to show that was the case: 1) when Alice signed the trust, 2) when she transferred a savings account into the trust, 3) when she refinanced the house owned by the trust, 4) when she named the trust as a beneficiary on her IRA, and 5) every other time she acted as a trustee or beneficiary of the trust. This can be stretched to also include every time she wrote a check from an account owned by her trust.

In particular, attorneys have to be extremely careful in recommending wills for domestic partners because of the comparatively high number of relatives willing to make trouble over an estate. It is probably much safer to establish a revocable living trust and properly fund it for no other reason than to help deter challenges in the future.

While these three reasons—high settlement costs, delay and contestability—are all valid points to recommend using a revocable living trust to avoid probate, there are many more reasons to use a revocable living trust. In fact, an entire book has been written on this subject. For the foremost non-legal text on revocable living trusts, please read *The Living Trust* by Henry Abts III from McGraw-Hill.

By now, you hopefully have the right impression that probate is something to be avoided. Unless there is no one you trust to take care of your last wishes and you refuse to appoint a trust company, then there is no need for the probate court to be involved. There are a few ways to avoid probate, but some carry their own risks and costs. Of course, I'm referring to joint property and beneficiary designations.

Planning Mistake #2: Using Joint Property

Whenever two people commit themselves to each other, they invariably get around to discussing how their home is titled. If one person owns the home, the person wants the partner to feel he or she has equal ownership in the house. So the natural urge is to re-title the house in both partners' names with a right of survivorship. Simple? Yes. Effective? *No.*

What joint property fails to account for is the federal gift tax that allows only the first $12,000 (in the year this book was published) given from one person to another without the tax being imposed. Every dollar after that is subject to a gift tax. However, the federal government, in all of its renowned mercy, graciously allows $1 million to be gifted over the course of your life without you actually having to pay the tax. The downside is it also lowers the amount dollar-for-dollar you are allowed to pass on without estate taxes upon death.

Before we get to an example, and before you tune out completely because of the million dollar exemption, the real danger here is not the actual payment of tax, but the failure to file a gift tax form with the IRS. Because of two of the IRS's favorite words "interest" and "penalties," it is best to stay above board on all of these transactions. The other reason for reading on and keeping gifts to less than $12,000 a year is to avoid having to recreate records when the IRS audits a person's estate and finds multiple gifts without a gift tax form being filled out. If you record all transactions properly and avoid situations where gifts of $12,000 or more per year are made between partners, then you can prevent huge accounting bills in the event of IRS action.

Please note this is only related to federal gift taxes. My own home state of North Carolina imposes a gift tax on every dollar above $12,000 gifted between domestic partners in a given year. For more information on how the gift tax may affect you in your own state, please see a qualified accountant or CPA in your area for specific tax advice.

Now, for the example:

Andy and Barney are partners, and they decide to live in Barney's home. Instead of talking to a life and estate planning attorney, Barney talks to his brother's mechanic's sister-in-law who used to work as a real estate loan processor, and who tells Barney to just do a general warranty deed saying Andy and Barney own the house as joint tenants with a right of survivorship. Depending on the real estate attorney Barney gets to handle the deed, he or she may not even know or care about gift taxes. Barney's house and land are worth $400,000, so half of it is a gift from Barney to Andy.

Looking at the numbers, the $200,000 gift was made from Barney to Andy. The first $12,000 is exempt in that year, so provided Barney does not make any more taxable gifts to Andy, there is a gift of $188,000 to be reported. If this is the first time Barney has to report any taxable gifts in excess of $12,000, then we can deduct the $188,000 from Barney's lifetime gift exemptions of $1 million, and $722,000 remains that Barney can still gift during his life. You also have to deduct the $188,000 from the $1 million post 2011 that Barney can pass to others without estate taxes when he dies. That leaves $722,000 Barney can leave to others when he passes on.

The procedure for Barney to report these gifts is to fill out a federal gift tax form, currently Form 709, as well as any gift tax forms his state requires. He should also keep a running total of all gifts given so he does not unintentionally give more than $1 million in taxable gifts during his life and would then have to lay out cash to pay the gift tax. The gift tax does not only apply to land, but everything else of value as well, such as stock and other accounts.

Another drawback to joint property with a right of survivorship is it only looks one step ahead. When one partner passes on, the other will receive the property, but what happens if both partners pass on together or within a short amount of time of each other? The property will have to go through probate before it can be distributed to the intended beneficiaries. Good life and estate planning looks more than one step ahead to cover multiple contingencies and avoid probate for all

To receive a free gift worth $39.97, please go to
www.estateplanningfordomesticpartners.com/gift

of them. With the right revocable living trust, the property can be titled in the name of the trust, all of these contingencies can be spelled out, and the property will go where it was intended without probate.

Let's use an example to cure the referenced drawbacks of joint property. Rather than use joint property with a right of survivorship, Barney and Andy decide to create a joint revocable living trust with an integrated separate property agreement (which may be a Partner AB-SECURE™ Trust). Andy places the house into the trust and lists it as separate property belonging to him.

Now the house is owned by the trust, both Andy and Barney are equal trustees and owners of the trust, but the domestic partner property agreement keeps the property technically separate for gift tax purposes. It is also listed the house will go to Barney if Andy passes on, and if Barney passes on first then it will go to his nephew Greg. If Greg passes on, it will go to his cousin Peter. If Peter also passes on, it will go to his friend Bobby. And if Bobby passes on, it will go equally to his sisters Marcia, Jan and Cindy. Now the property not only avoids the gift tax problems associated with joint property, but it now lists multiple levels of beneficiaries who would receive the property upon death without the property having to go through probate.

Planning Mistake #3: Beneficiary Designations

In an effort to make things simple and avoid probate on accounts and life insurance, many institutions allow their clients to name beneficiaries on the accounts, and many even allow a place to indicate a contingent beneficiary. While this is good for the client, it is also good for the company because now it is not in the middle of a probate proceeding that may be contested. Legally, the company is fulfilling its obligation after the death of the client once it transfers the account to the new named owner. In most cases, and depending on the company, it is a quick process taking a few days to handle the paperwork and make the transfer.

While beneficiary designations are not as lethal to some plans as wills and joint property with a right of survivorship, there are still some drawbacks to using beneficiary designations rather than a revocable living trust. As mentioned before with joint property, it only accounts for one transfer upon the death of the owner. If and when the owner passes on, it will go to the person or persons listed as the beneficiary. What if that person passes on before them? Financial institutions which allow for contingent beneficiaries have let the client take care of the first "what if" by listing a contingent beneficiary, but what if this beneficiary passes on as well?

By using a revocable living trust, all of the different contingencies can be listed within the trust, and now the account is handled properly, without probate, regardless of how many years pass by and how many different people may have passed on. Depending on the type of account, the account can either be placed into the trust directly or the beneficiary designation features on the account can name the trust as the beneficiary upon death. Now the account can stay in the individual partner's name during life and name the trust as beneficiary upon death. The different methods of funding a revocable living trust include changing beneficiary designations the right way, and these techniques are covered more fully in Chapter Eight.

There is another serious drawback to using beneficiary designations, and the best way to illustrate this is through an example and a simple question.

Alice and Vera have a son, Tommy, who is 18. Alice and Vera each have managed to accumulate assets. Aside from the family home, their biggest assets are two brokerage accounts worth $500,000 each. One belongs to Alice and the other belongs to Vera, so Alice lists Vera as her primary beneficiary on the account and Vera lists Alice. Both list their son Tommy as contingent beneficiary. Vera and Alice are involved in a car accident and both pass on. Tommy will now receive their brokerage accounts, without probate. Now for the question—what do you think 18 year-old Tommy is going to do with the $1 million?

Most parents understand that while they love their children and they may be legal adults at 18, most 18 year olds are not responsible enough to effectively handle a large inheritance. By placing a child's name on a beneficiary designation, the child gets control of the account at age 18, should anything happen to the parent. If instead, a revocable living trust was listed as the beneficiary, a trustee would manage this account for Tommy's benefit until he reaches a more suitable age. Alice and Vera could plan ahead by naming a succession of trustees to handle things and choose the age of distribution, such as when Tommy turns 25 or 30 years of age.

We have now covered three of the biggest life and estate planning mistakes, as well as the reasons why they are mistakes. You have also seen there is hope for successful planning. The main method for avoiding the problems outlined here is covered in the chapters devoted to the revocable living trust. In many situations, it is exactly what domestic partners need as the core of their life and estate plans. Before we cover revocable living trusts in more detail in Chapters Five through Ten, we will look at some of the basic documents needed for domestic partners to effectively create a life and estate plan.

Chapter Three:
Healthcare Directives

One of the most common horror stories for domestic partners revolves around one partner falling ill and the other not being allowed to make medical decisions, or worse, not even being allowed to visit the partner in the hospital. The number of stories is vast, and it is profoundly disturbing that a partner of 40 years is suddenly swept aside in favor of long-estranged relatives to make medical decisions.

There has been a lot of bad advice out there in certain aspects of life and estate planning, but thankfully one of those areas has not been about healthcare powers of attorney and living wills. Perhaps due to the horror stories as well as to the lack of legal rights and societal acceptance, gay and lesbian couples have been ahead of unmarried couples in embracing these documents. The healthcare power of attorney allows a person to appoint agents to make healthcare decisions when he or she is not able to do so. These decisions can encompass everything from the simple choice of whether either brand-name or generic aspirin should be given to the patient, up to the gut-wrenching decision of whether or not life support should be withdrawn.

A living will (sometimes referred to as an advance healthcare directive), contains specific orders from the patient, written in advance, regarding course of treatment if the person is in a persistent vegetative state, is terminal and incurable or is considered by the state to be incapable of giving informed consent. Some states use a living will less as your own orders and more as a specific appointment of someone to make just life support decisions for you.

A complete set of directives should include a healthcare power of attorney and living will. These directives should address the following areas:

- A successive list of the people; i.e., your agents, to make healthcare decisions for you

- When the power of attorney agent is allowed to make decisions for you

- How the power of attorney is rescinded

- The general and specific statements of the authority granted

- A statement regarding any powers which are specifically *not* granted to the power of attorney

- Clauses limiting liability for medical professionals as well as third parties if they rely on the power of attorney

- Directions on how to proceed if you are on life support and artificial nutrition and there is no hope of recovery.

Healthcare Power of Attorney (HPOA)

Before going into the specifics of a healthcare power of attorney, it is important to note different states have different rules, and your state's rules may be different. Something that is universal among all 50 states is if you do not have a healthcare power of attorney, then the state provides you with one, and it is usually your "next of kin." These various state statutes are what give relatives precedence over a domestic partner in making medical decisions because, once again, you are not legally married. (Thankfully at the time of this writing, this is not the case in Massachusetts, since gay and lesbian couples are allowed to marry, but family members are the next "next of kin" after your partner.) Whether you reside in the Bay State or not, you may have other people you wish to name as alternate agents instead of abiding by your state's definition of next of kin. That is why everyone, even married couples, should have these documents.

Choosing your healthcare agents

The primary decision when putting together a healthcare power of attorney is choosing who will be your agents. The best piece of advice I can give is to name only one person at a time. A central reason for a healthcare power of attorney is to make it absolutely clear who is making decisions if you cannot do it yourself. Naming two or three people to act together is a recipe for discord and confusion. Imagine a doctor having a healthcare power of attorney with three agents listed as acting together. The doctor gets an order from one agent, a second agent shows up and gives a contradictory order, and then the third shows up and wants the doctor to do something completely different. Having one agent acting at a time solves this problem by having one clear voice to speak on your behalf at this critical time.

I know what some of you are thinking. "Well, after my partner, I have three children (or nieces or nephews, or brothers and sisters, etc.) and I don't want any of them to feel left out. I love them all equally."

As an attorney who has been counseling clients for more than a decade on powers of attorney, I understand the arguments. But what we are talking about is your health and your life—not whether or not one person got a better Christmas present, or whether or not you gave one of them more money over the years, and certainly not whom you love best. At this most critical of times, you need to select the best person for the job first, the second best person for the job second, and so on. It has nothing to do with loving people unequally, and it has everything to do with choosing the person who will be the best healthcare agent for you.

So who would be the best healthcare agent? Domestic partners usually know their partner is first on their list, but where they run into trouble is selecting the successor agents. I usually give my clients a little direction on choosing their agents. Choose someone who:

- generally thinks the way you do about medical decisions and healthcare

- is medically knowledgeable, or at least is medically curious and will look into your situation

- has no trouble seeking a second opinion or firing a doctor.

Considering someone who generally thinks the way you do on medical decisions and healthcare can give a little or a lot of weight in choosing or denying certain people as your agent. For some people, this may mean choosing trusted people in your particular religion so they can make medical decisions in line with your religious practices. In other cases, it may mean you wish to rely on prescription medication as little as possible and therefore you want someone knowledgeable about alternative medicines. The main point is to pick someone who generally thinks as you do regarding medicine.

The second factor is making sure your agents are medically knowledgeable, or at least medically curious. The second part of that sentence is probably more important than the first. The person you want making medical decisions for you should take the time to look into the medical treatments recommended, do some research, and then ask intelligent questions of the doctor, possibly even challenging the physician. Recent studies suggest there are an appalling number of times a doctor or nurse administers the wrong medication or the wrong dose, sometimes resulting in medical tragedies or death. It is important you have a healthcare agent who will be an informed second set of eyes making sure everything runs smoothly as you recover.

Finally, your healthcare agent should be bold enough to stand up to a doctor, get a second opinion if he or she thinks it is warranted, and be able to fire a doctor if necessary. It does you no good to choose a person who thinks as you do, will look into medical matters to make sure everything is going well, but if he realizes something is wrong, he is too timid to bring it up with the doctor. You don't need someone who is belligerent, but at the same time, the person should not be afraid to get a second opinion.

Let's take a look at how one partner, Will, may choose his healthcare agents.

Will and his partner Vince are choosing healthcare agents, and while they agree Will should be Vince's first agent and vice-versa, they have completely different views on who should be their successor agents. Will has a best friend Grace, and while she understands how Will would think on medical decisions, he does not think Grace has a lot of healthcare knowledge and may not look into matters as much as others might. While Grace will probably be on the list, she is not necessarily the first successor agent. His friend Karen has an extensive background in prescription medication, she certainly has no problem standing up to a doctor, and when it comes down to it she will do what is best for Will. Jack is a good friend of Will's but would probably be one of the worst agents possible, thinking because he played a doctor on stage once, he knows more than the real doctors do.

In looking at his options, Will expands his list of prospects a little and realizes Grace's mother Bobbi is probably the best choice because of her tenacity, her ability to look into healthcare information, and the fact she cares about him as if he were her own son. He then names Karen as his alternate agent, and Grace as his second alternate agent. His list of healthcare power of attorney agents now looks like this:

1) Vince

2) Bobbi

3) Karen

4) Grace

Choosing the healthcare agents is typically the hardest part of formulating a healthcare power of attorney. Although we outlined the other components of the document and will cover them in this chapter, it is usually recommended you give the agent the maximum amount of power allowed so he or she can have the flexibility to do what is best for you.

When Power of Attorney agents should act

In order for a healthcare agent to start making decisions for you, you have to be no longer able to make decisions for yourself. So, breathe a little easier. By creating a power of attorney for healthcare decisions, you are not giving up your right to make those decisions yourself. It is only if you are not able to make decisions or communicate them that you let someone else make the decisions for you.

But when are you considered to be "not able" or "incapacitated" for these purposes? The power of attorney would outline the conditions, or if not, then state law would decide when you are incapacitated. In general, it is preferable for you to determine in the healthcare power of attorney exactly what triggers the power of attorney to act. The alternative may be a court proceeding in which a judge has to weigh evidence and testimony, and that may be a costly, complicated procedure.

Most healthcare powers of attorney, even the office supply store versions, will list the conditions under which the power of attorney is active. It may be as simple as stating if "any attending physician" certifies in writing you are not able to make your own healthcare wishes known, then the power of attorney becomes active and your agent can act on your behalf.

There are also some choices available to you in the power of attorney document. You may also specifically designate one or more physicians to make the determination. If you have had the same doctor for 20 years and feel comfortable with him or her, then you may want that physician to specifically make that determination. But this choice also comes with a word of caution. It may be a longer procedure than you think, and it may be expensive to have your regular physician make the diagnosis if you are on the other side of the country when the diagnosis is needed. You should always weigh the comfort you have with a particular physician against the flexibility which may be needed in given situations. If my clients are given any guidance, almost all decide to keep things flexible and simply state any two attending physicians may make this certification in writing.

How a Power of Attorney is rescinded

Just as important as when a healthcare power of attorney is active is when and how it is revoked. Just as "when" an agent may act is written in the document, the method of revoking the power of attorney should also be written into it.

While the process may be as elaborate as having to execute a new power of attorney, it is recommended you keep it simpler than that. The process also should not be so simple that there are no formalities at all, such as saying "I revoke my healthcare power of attorney." Having things this simple opens the door to meddling family members lying and declaring you verbally rescinded your power of attorney in a "moment of clarity." Now all of the court proceedings you hoped to avoid can spring up. The simplest balance is to have the revocation of a healthcare power of attorney in writing.

To receive a free gift worth $39.97, please go to
www.estateplanningfordomesticpartners.com/gift

Authorities granted to your agent

Now that you have appointed healthcare agents and decided when the power of attorney is active and rescinded, it is time to determine exactly what authority your agent will have. In general, it is recommended his or her powers be extensive so the individual can handle any situation that arises. Each healthcare power of attorney should list at least the following powers:

- Information — the ability to receive and review medical records; the ability to consent to the disclosure of medical records; and the ability to sign all consent and other forms necessary to carry out the other powers

- Manage Health Professionals — the ability to hire and fire medical professionals; the ability to admit and discharge you from medical facilities; and the ability to consent or withhold consent for all medications and procedures

- Releases — Clauses limiting liability for medical professionals, as well as third parties if they rely on the power of attorney

- Life Support — the ability to authorize or withhold life support and other treatment if you are in certain terminal and incurable conditions.

Information

One of the most important clauses of a healthcare power of attorney is the ability to receive and review medical records. After all, it does you and your partner no good to have all of the other powers if the partner has nothing on which to base his or her decision. It is also critical your partner be allowed to release the medical records to other medical practitioners so her or she can make their best recommendations and care for you.

Imagine a doctor asking you to approve an operation for you partner, but the doctor cannot disclose any medical information to you, explain why it is necessary, or what the possible risks and side effects would be. I can't imagine approving the repair of my car without all of the facts, let alone making a decision about someone's health.

Part of granting this authority should also specifically include a waiver of privacy rights under the Health Insurance Portability and Accountability Act of 1996. The law, while good for patient privacy on many levels, also put roadblocks in place that made most healthcare powers of attorney ineffective by denying healthcare agents access to necessary medical information. My firm includes HIPAA waiver language in all of our powers of attorney, but The Estate Plan and some other attorneys prefer to execute waivers as a separate form. Either method works to give your agent the authority he or she needs to take care of your health.

It is also important to include the power to sign all consent forms on your behalf, and this is probably the power that will be utilized most often. In an age where medicine is governed by bureaucracy, there are many forms to sign, so it is standard practice to give your healthcare agent the broadest possible authority to sign consent forms.

Manage health professionals

The ability to receive or refuse medical treatment and the ability to engage and discharge medical professionals are hallmarks of our healthcare system. If you believe your doctor is not acting competently or if you just don't like the doctor, you always have the ability to fire him or her. If you want to try an experimental treatment or if you object to receiving blood transfusions, you have the right to consent to or refuse specific medical treatments and medications. And if you are unable to exercise these rights, it is critical that your agent exercise them for you.

Part of being able to manage health professionals also includes the power to admit and discharge you from hospitals, nursing facilities and other places of medical treatment. If you admit yourself to a hospital and, because of the negligence of the hospital you become incapacitated, you would want your partner to be able to get you out of that hospital and into a new one as quickly as possible.

Releases

Some important terms for making sure orders given by your partner and other healthcare agents are obeyed are clauses releasing medical professionals, hospitals and others from any and all liability for obeying your agent. The main concern here is doctors and hospitals do not want to be sued for following your healthcare agent's order.

Imagine a situation where you were involved in a car accident and are unconscious. The emergency room doctors examine you and determine you need one of two operations to save your life. One, if successful, is 100 percent likely to save your life but it involves amputating your leg. The other, which the doctors recommend, is 80 percent likely to save your life and does not involve any amputations. Your healthcare agent wants to authorize the first operation with the amputation.

At this point, the doctors, hospital and others involved in providing medical care are worried once you regain consciousness you will sue them for the amputation of your leg. In order to make it easy for them to accept the orders of your chosen agent without question or seeking a court order to follow their directions, they want to confirm they will not be held liable for obeying your agent's orders. For this reason, extensive language is usually incorporated into healthcare powers of attorney releasing just about everyone from liability for obeying your agent. This language does not release anyone from liability for being negligent or for medical malpractice, only from being liable for following instructions of the healthcare agent.

Life support

Another component of a healthcare power of attorney is a general statement about life support and artificial nutrition. Many people do not want to be "hooked up to machines" or "fed through a tube" if there is no hope of recovery. Others want to hang on for as long as technology will s their body functioning. It does not matter which choice you make as long as you also list these wishes in writing in the power of attorney.

Writing out these wishes will give your agents and physicians clear direction on what you want to have done. It is then up to your agent to authorize your wishes and the medical professionals to carry out the wishes. The other way to handle this difficult decision is to make it ahead of time in a living will.

Living Will

The living will may be the simplest document in a life and estate plan, but it may turn out to be the most important one for your partner and loved ones to have. Although the healthcare power of attorney allows your partner and others to make medical decisions for you, the living will takes the final, most difficult decision out of their hands. When it comes to whether or not to administer life support and artificial nutrition and hydration at the end of life, a living will can express your wishes and directions.

There are two very powerful reasons to have a living will. First, it expresses your wishes should you ever get to the point where doctors would ask if they should "pull the plug." Actually, doctors have much more tactful ways of expressing things in these situations, but we can get right to the point. What you want in this situation is not clear unless you have it in writing, and a living will does that for you.

The second reason for having a living will is for the benefit of your partner, friends and family members. By placing your orders to a doctor in writing and in the proper format under state law, you take the burden of making that decision from your loved ones. In legal terms, the living will overrides your healthcare power of attorney because it is a specific document with a specific order for a specific situation, and, depending on the state, can be taken right from the statutes.

It is important to note most states allow a living will to make the determination ahead of time, so as long as your attending physicians (or even a specific doctor chosen by you) determines there is no hope of recovery and your body is only being kept going by machines, then your wishes will be followed. Other states do not allow this kind of order to be made and instead insist a person chosen by you make the decision for you at the time. Until those states catch up with the others, you can still make your wishes known in a living will, but your chosen agent will have to make the decision for you.

How the Living Will works with the Healthcare Power of Attorney

By using a healthcare power of attorney, you have most likely stated your wishes are covered by a living will. Either you want life support and artificial nutrition or not. But this is merely language to give your agent direction should you ever fall that ill. The living will is an *order* from you on what needs to be done, signed under the formalities imposed by state law, and should be presented to the doctors directly.

In short, the healthcare power of attorney covers all healthcare decisions you would be able to make yourself except for the last, most difficult one. That decision is expressed in your living will. *Not even your healthcare power of attorney agent can override your decision.*

It is with this last part that some couples, whether married or not, express some reservations. There is quite naturally conflict between the desire to take this incredible burden off your partner and make the decision ahead of time, and yet there is a desire to not let your partner feel helpless to stop doctors from removing medical treatment that is keeping your body functioning. In these situations, the decision comes down to whether or not to have a living will at all. If there is no living will, then your designated agent makes the decision for you.

Let's use an example. Felix and Oscar are partners, and they generally trust each other's judgment. In putting together their healthcare documents, they name each other as their healthcare agents first, and then they both name their friend Murray as a second agent. They each name their former wives third. Felix feels Oscar (and all of the other agents) would be able to make decisions regarding life support and would prefer to trust Oscar's judgment. Oscar believes Felix becomes too emotional in these tough situations and would be unable to act, and he simply does not want to burden any of the other agents with this responsibility. Therefore, they agree Oscar will have a living will and Felix will simply state his wishes in his healthcare power of attorney, trusting Oscar and the other agents to act if necessary.

Combining the Healthcare Power of Attorney and the Living Will

Some attorneys use a single standard document to cover all of the items in a healthcare power of attorney and a living will. There is certainly no prohibition against doing this, but our firm and The Estate Plan prefer to keep these documents separate.

Doctors are typically very busy people and would prefer not to look through extensive documents if it can be done more simply. If the situation calls for the language contained in a living will, then the doctor does not have to sift through all of the other language in a healthcare power of attorney to find what he or she needs to know. If the doctor needs to make sure the healthcare agent can give the type of order required, then the doctor can look through the healthcare power of attorney without the language of the living will getting in the way.

Will doctors honor these documents?

I would like to say doctors and hospitals will follow the law, but it is not always the case. The law *requires* doctors to follow the directives in a healthcare power of attorney and living will, but sometimes doctors ignore the law and turn to the next of kin, out of habit, convenience or prejudice. In these cases, it is important for your partner or other agent to make it very clear he or she will institute legal action to have your documents enforced. (Again, this is another reason to choose a healthcare agent who will stand up to a doctor). A court can review the documents and issue an order forcing the doctor to accept the orders of your directives.

Nomination of conservator

Another important document to have as part of your life and estate plan is a document that nominates your conservator. A conservator is a court appointed guardian. In the event you are unable to handle your own matters, your power of attorney document *should* be all you need to make sure the people you choose handle your healthcare and other matters. However, it is still possible for a judge to stretch his or her authority and start a proceeding to assign you a conservator.

If that happens, it is critical you have a list of conservators in writing *you* prefer. If you have conservators listed, it becomes even harder for a judge to select someone else without a good reason. It is also good practice to make the people you nominated as healthcare power of attorney agents to be the same people nominated as conservators. The jobs are nearly identical, and the criteria for naming a healthcare agent are the same for choosing a conservator. Again, this may be another spare tire, but it is better to have it and not need it than to need it and not have it.

Summary

Compared to married couples, domestic partners are at a disadvantage when it comes to making medical decisions for each other, but the playing field is leveled with a properly drafted healthcare power of attorney. By making sure all of the main powers and clauses we discussed are in your medical documents, you and your partner can rest easier knowing you are now legally able to address these issues should they arise.

Chapter Four:
Financial Power of Attorney

While there are many horror stories about partners not being able to make healthcare decisions for each other, there are just as many that involve a partner falling ill, the estranged family stepping in and before you know it, the other partner is out on the street. This is a particularly difficult situation if the partner who falls ill is the provider and the other is the homemaker. Unless legal steps are taken, the family members, as heartless as they may be, could be well within their legal rights to do just that.

The easiest solution for partners is to name each other as agents in their financial power of attorney documents. As power of attorney, the partner can manage the assets of the sick partner and still have access to their home and finances without worrying the "next of kin" will be able to go to court and take over. But just in case they do take matters to court, it is also recommended partners execute a nomination of a conservator or similar document so if a judge feels compelled to give someone legal "guardianship" over your partner, then your partner has a list of people he or she would choose.

Financial documents should have a financial power of attorney and a nomination of a conservator, and between them they should address the following areas:

- a successive list of the people to make financial decisions for you

- when the power of attorney agent can act

To receive a free gift worth $39.97, please go to
www.estateplanningfordomesticpartners.com/gift

- general and specific statements of the authority granted

- statement regarding any powers specifically *not* granted to the power of attorney

- clauses limiting liability for financial institutions as well as third parties if they rely on the power of attorney

- nominations of conservators if a proceeding is instituted to assign one.

This list should look vaguely familiar when compared to the chapter on healthcare directives. This is because the same elements need to go into both healthcare and financial powers of attorney even though they are covering two very different areas.

Financial Power of Attorney (FPOA)

There are many names for a financial power of attorney. A nondurable power of attorney, a durable power of attorney or a springing power of attorney are some terms you may have heard. These and other specially named powers of attorney refer to the same exact powers; the names refer to when they are active.

A nondurable power of attorney is active while the principal, meaning the person whose power of attorney it is, is competent. It becomes inactive if the principal is deemed incompetent. (In 10 years of handling life and estate planning matters, I have never had a client who wanted this type of power of attorney, since people generally want someone to act for them if they can't. But it is out there.) A durable power of attorney, sometimes called a general power of attorney, refers to a power of attorney that is active while the principal is competent and then also remains active after a person becomes incompetent. A springing power of attorney only becomes active after the principal becomes incapacitated.

To receive a free gift worth $39.97, please go to
www.estateplanningfordomesticpartners.com/gift

To keep things simple and understandable, we will avoid using these terms and instead generally call these documents financial powers of attorney. As for when they are active, we will also specifically discuss this since many clients want a blend of the durable and springing power of attorney, depending on which agent is named.

Choosing your financial agents

The most important part of drafting a financial power of attorney is deciding who will make decisions for you. As with the healthcare power of attorney, I also recommend only naming one person at a time to avoid conflicting decisions or needing more than one person to sign documents to get things done for you. While you may want your partner and your brother to work together to make financial decisions, it may be next to impossible to have them go to the bank together each and every time something needs to be signed.

Who would make good financial power of attorney agents? Partners usually name each other first, and then I generally advise my clients to agree on an agent who:

- is a person they trust with their assets and their life

- is financially knowledgeable but not necessarily an accountant or financial advisor

- knows when it is time to get financial help and can work with professionals.

The first criterion is the most important, because if you cannot trust the person with your money and your livelihood, then there is no need to look into the other two factors. While there are many financially qualified people who can do a good job at managing your finances if you fall ill, you first have to trust the person.

Second is to select someone who is financially knowledgeable but not necessarily an accountant or financial advisor. If the person can balance a checkbook and make practical decisions in spending money, then that is good enough. You are not asking your financial power of attorney agent to do your taxes or create an investment portfolio. You are only asking him or her to handle your bills, preserve your assets, and work with the right professionals to get those items done.

Finally, you should jointly choose a financial power of attorney agent who knows when it is time to hire a professional to help. There are people who are "chronic do-it-yourselfers." They may insist on handling all aspects of your finances, even those things you usually passed off to your CPA or financial advisor, out of stubbornness or a belief that by doing it themselves they are saving you money. Unfortunately, they could end up placing your finances in jeopardy. The agent you want is someone who can handle the everyday spending decisions and manage the professionals to keep your finances moving and growing while you are ill.

Let's go back to our friend Will from the earlier chapter and see how he and Vince choose financial agents versus the healthcare agents they chose.

Will clearly wants his partner Vince to handle all of his financial matters if he becomes ill (and vice-versa), but they also want to make sure if anything happens to the other there are backup agents in place. Grace may become overly emotional when it comes to healthcare matters, but by and large she is good about finances. Will and Vince discuss this and feel with the right financial advice she would be able to handle matters for them, and they both trust her.

Will selected Karen as one of his healthcare agents because of her medical knowledge. However, she can't help but spend money needlessly. Will and Vince feel if Vince died and Will went into a coma for a few months, he would wake up in a gold-plated hospital bed, an apartment full of appliances from QVC, and all of his bank accounts emptied. Clearly, Karen should not be on their list of agents. If Jack were their agent, all of the money would be gone without any explanation at all, so Jack is also out.

In looking at the people they know and trust, they know if it were necessary, Ben, Will's boss at his old law firm, would take care of things. If all else failed, they know they can also depend on the trust company their financial advisor works with, XYZ Trust Company. While this may be a more expensive option, Will and Vince know the company would do a good job for what they are paid.

In looking at who they trust, who has financial ability and knowledge, and who will get help when needed, Will and Vince jointly decide to go with the following power of attorney agents:

1) Vince for Will and Will for Vince

2) Grace

3) Ben

4) XYZ Trust Company

The hardest part of creating a financial power of attorney is now done. In most cases, the rest of the power of attorney language is standard and there is not a lot of customization needs to be done, but be sure it includes all of the other elements mentioned.

To receive a free gift worth $39.97, please go to
www.estateplanningfordomesticpartners.com/gift

In addition, make sure your attorney does not prepare powers of attorney for you and your partner are commonly called "short form" powers of attorney. In many cases, including my home state of North Carolina, there have been court actions that deny agents certain powers because they were not adequately spelled out in the document. A short form is a quick list of powers that is not elaborated, and so when it comes to some specific actions an agent wants to take, judges have been reluctant to allow them.

When a Power of Attorney agent should act

As mentioned before, there are three main time frames for when a power of attorney agent can act—both while you are competent and incompetent, only after you become incompetent and not before, or only while you are competent and not if you become incompetent. In determining when your agents should act, you should keep these situations in mind.

For most domestic partners, when they name each other as the first agent, there is value in having a durable power of attorney, which is active both now and if one becomes incapacitated. This allows domestic partners to act for each other the same married couples do. If the cable bill is in Will's name and the telephone account is under Vince's, each can make changes because they are the power of attorney. For more time sensitive matters, if Vince has to suddenly go out of town and they are scheduled to refinance their home, Will can simply use the power of attorney and sign for both. If one becomes incapacitated, then the other partner can continue to handle the couple's financial transactions.

While it is convenient for domestic partners to name each other as their first agents and have the power of attorney active all of the time, this is not necessarily what the partners want for successor agents. It is more common for people to want a successor agent to act only if they are unable to handle things themselves. For example, partners Gomez and Morticia may want to name each other as their primary power of attorney agents and have their documents active now and also if they become incapacitated. They may also trust Gomez's brother Fester and their friend Lurch, but they do not necessarily want them to have their powers active as long as they are still able to handle things themselves.

For Gomez, he would list his power of attorney agents as:

1) Morticia, active now and also upon incapacity

2) Fester, only active upon incapacity

3) Lurch, only upon incapacity

This means Morticia may use the power of attorney at any time. If Morticia is deceased or unable to act as Gomez's agent, then Fester may act as Gomez's agent *only* if Gomez is incapacitated. Lurch may likewise only act as Gomez's agent if both Morticia and Fester cannot act as Gomez's agent *and* Gomez is incapacitated. Unless the people named before as agents are unable to act, the later-named agents cannot act as the power of attorney agent.

What does incapacitated mean?

Determining if the power of attorney is active can depend on whether or not someone is incapacitated. Exactly what does "incapacitated" mean? State laws vary on what this means, and states have different procedures to determine whether or not someone is incapacitated. But most of those procedures involve some court action, and that is precisely what we want to avoid. Instead, we can define "incapacitated" in the document itself.

In all cases, you want to make sure the definition of incapacitated is simple enough that it does not require a court to declare you incompetent, but at the same time it should be based upon solid medical evidence. The Estate Plan uses the following language in some of their power of attorney documents to define incapacity: "Principal shall be deemed incapacitated if at any time two (2) licensed physicians certify in writing that Principal has become physically or mentally disabled and is unable to manage his affairs in his best interest, whether or not a court of competent jurisdiction has declared Principal disabled, mentally ill or in need of a conservator/guardian."

The language does not have exact medical parameters, but it is clear any time two physicians state you can't take care of things yourself and put their determination in writing, you are incapacitated and unable to handle things yourself. It is also just as easy to determine you are competent to handle things again when two physicians certify in writing you are once again competent.

Authorities granted to your agent

We've looked at choosing financial agents and how and when the powers of attorney are active. Now we should look at the powers granted to the agent and what they can do on your behalf. In general, it is recommended financial powers be extensive so your agent can address issues as they arise. At a minimum, the document should list the following powers:

- general powers granted by statute

- handle tax matters

- make gifts

- change beneficiaries or re-title accounts or other assets

- purchase insurance or other financial products

General powers granted by statute

State laws usually spell out a list of powers a power of attorney agent or conservator can exercise, but most state laws do not cover everything needed. Nonetheless, it is a good idea to reference these powers as being part of the power of attorney. From this base, you can always add more powers.

Handle tax matters

An important part of being a power of attorney agent is handling all of your tax matters, including a few items that might not be incorporated into a general statement of authority or your state's statutes. In addition to simply being able to fill out and file tax returns, your agent should be able to get copies of past returns, settle any debts with the IRS or the state's department of revenue, file extensions, and claim refunds. In short, everything you can do as a taxpayer to interact with various government authorities should be included as part of the power of attorney.

Make gifts

While this may seem like something you would not want your power of attorney agent to do, it is actually critical he or she be allowed to if you were ever severely disabled and needed nursing home or similar care. As domestic partners, you are not able to claim certain exemptions as married couples would, and if you needed long-term care, you would have to exhaust your assets before Medicaid and other programs would take over the payments. (This is also a reason why we recommend our clients look into long-term care insurance).

While the rules are pretty strict regarding gifts, if there is time to transfer your assets to your partner using the power of attorney, you may be able to save some of those assets from having to be sold to pay for the long-term care facility. As a word of caution, do not try to handle applying for Medicaid or other programs without the assistance of an attorney or other professional who knows the rules. It can be extremely easy to make a costly mistake, so paying an attorney to help is well worth the price to save some of your assets.

Domestic partners may also wish to have this power to equalize their assets, even if one partner is incapacitated, to avoid future estate taxes. This topic is covered more fully in Chapter Fourteen, but for now it simply adds to the reasons in having your power of attorney incorporate gifting powers.

Change beneficiaries and re-title accounts

This power is particularly important if you and your partner have a revocable living trust and you need to change beneficiaries or title to property to fully fund your trust. In order to avoid probate, it is important your trust own your assets or list your trust as a "pay on death" or similar beneficiary.

If assets are in your individual name and need to be in the trust, then your agent needs the ability to re-title the asset by changing the account ownership or executing a new deed. If an asset like life insurance is still listing a person (even your partner) as your beneficiary, then the beneficiary would need to be changed to your revocable living trust. This topic is covered in more detail in Chapter Eight.

Purchase insurance or other financial products

Just as with gifting, it may be in your and your partner's best interests to have this power in your document in case you need long-term or nursing home care. To make things simple and to preserve your assets, your agent could liquidate some of your assets and purchase an insurance annuity. An annuity is simply a type of life insurance with an investment portfolio attached to it which can be "annuitized."

When an annuity is annuitized, the insurance is cancelled with the company keeping all of the investments but in exchange they agree to pay you a set amount each month for the remainder of your life, no matter how long that may be. Your power of attorney agent can work with the insurance company to buy an annuity that will provide a monthly payment which covers all of your long-term care costs, and then the rest of your assets can be reserved for your partner.

While some of these situations may seem far-fetched right now, there is little reason to take these powers out of the documents just because you think it might not happen to you or your partner. When explaining some of these powers and other protective language to our clients, we usually call them "spare tire" clauses. Just because you don't expect to get a flat tire on the way to the grocery store does not mean you take the spare tire out of the car. It's there if you need it, and if you don't need it, then it's simply words on paper.

Statement regarding any powers specifically not granted to the power of attorney

While in most cases there are very few powers you should deny your agent, the option is there for you. In practice, it is best to give your power of attorney agent as much authority as possible. It is also a good idea to have a section to list those powers even if your answer is "NONE," meaning there are no powers you are denying to your agent.

If you are choosing to exclude any powers from the document, be sure you understand precisely the powers you wish to exclude, the reasons for excluding the power, and the consequences of if you end up in a situation where that power is needed. Be sure to talk this through with your attorney when putting the document together since, if he or she is a good attorney, he or she would be able to give you some examples of why the power is needed.

Releases

Just as it is important to release medical professionals from liability for obeying the orders of your healthcare agent, it is just as important to release financial institutions from liability for listening to your power of attorney agent. Again, the financial or other institution wants to make sure you will not regain the ability to act for yourself and then sue them for taking the orders of your agent if something does not go exactly as planned.

If your stockbroker took an order from your agent to sell one stock and purchase another and the second stock tanked, the stockbroker would not want you to come back and sue them for making the transaction. Therefore, unless the stockbroker is assured her or she will not be held liable for the bad decisions of your agent, the stockbroker would never accept the power of attorney in the first place. To make sure your agent will be listened to and obeyed, it is essential to have this release language in the document.

Do not misunderstand the meaning of the release language. If your stockbroker did something negligent or reckless, or even stole from you, this language would not protect him or her. All this language does is prevent you from suing them because they took orders from your assigned power of attorney agent. It is nothing more than that.

To receive a free gift worth $39.97, please go to
www.estateplanningfordomesticpartners.com/gift

Summary

Financial powers of attorney are critical components of a domestic partner life and estate plan. Through them, you and your partner can establish even more power for each other than married couples get by signing a marriage certificate. It is critical to make sure your power of attorney is complete, so be sure to review these points with your attorney. For added protection, be sure you and your partner have nomination of conservator documents just in case a judge feels compelled to poke their way into your affairs.

SECTION II:
REVOCABLE LIVING TRUSTS

More than any other document or technique, a joint revocable living trust combined with a domestic partnership property agreement can help domestic partners achieve many of their goals. By finding the right professionals to work with and using the right trust and accompanying documents, domestic partners can truly gain many of the same rights as married couples. As a matter of fact, by planning appropriately, domestic partners can have more of what they want than married couples will ever have by signing a marriage certificate.

Chapter Five:
Coming Together Without Penalties
Through a Revocable Living Trust

Now it is time to move into some advanced planning for domestic partners. Solid healthcare and financial powers of attorney, a nomination of conservator and living will are all routine documents included in a good domestic partner life and estate plan. But a joint revocable living trust will form the core of your plan and be the main vehicle for avoiding many problems faced by couples in general and by domestic partners in particular.

Finding the right attorney

Many attorneys are familiar with revocable living trusts as a means of avoiding probate for their individual and married clients, but there are not a lot of attorneys who know how to successfully create a trust for domestic partners. Worse still, there are many attorneys who think they know what they are doing when it comes to life and estate planning in general, but in truth they only have a cursory knowledge and assume because they passed the bar exam, they know all they need to know.

Unlike other areas of law, it is difficult for an attorney to know if he or she did something wrong until it is too late to do anything about it. If a real estate transaction is messed up, there is a good chance someone will catch it before the closing. If an attorney messes up on procedure in a divorce, it is likely an opposing attorney, a clerk or the judge will point out this mistake. Unless another attorney proficient in life and estate planning reviews your documents, there is usually no one else in the process who would know what was wrong until the documents were needed. And once a person is deceased or incapacitated, there is little, if anything, that can be done.

It is always a good to sit down with an attorney and ask questions before hiring one. In order to help you find the right attorney and other professionals in putting together your life and estate plan, you and your partner should look for the following warning signs:

- They recommend using joint property with a right of survivorship and never mention gift taxes.

- They tell you all you need are wills and you shouldn't even discuss a trust.

- They say probate is not a big deal and their firm handles probate cases all of the time.

If you notice any of the above points, then they clearly do not have the knowledge to help you and your partner with life and estate planning. This is not to say they are bad lawyers, but I've often seen lawyers who are very good with real estate matters, or family law, or traffic court cases want to help when their clients come to them with another matter like drafting life and estate planning documents. The problem is they don't realize it is not that simple.

The summer after I turned 16, I went to work in a pizza place. Before I started working, I thought it couldn't be so difficult to make a pizza. What's involved, after all? You put it in the oven for a certain amount of time at a certain temperature, and then take it out, cut and serve. No big deal, right? Wrong.

Then I saw the process up close. You go from taking a ball of pizza dough kept at a certain temperature, to using just the right amount and mix of flour, to stretching the dough using just the right amount of pressure and movements, to placing the dough on a flat wooden board with a handle, to having just the right amount of raised dough at the edge to form a good crust, to putting just the right amount of sauce and cheese on the dough, to placing the board into the oven and giving it the right shaking movement to be able to pull the board out from under the pizza without stretching it into an oval, to cooking it just the right amount of time at 500 degrees, and then taking it out properly with a metal plate on a wooden handle, placing it on a metal plate for serving, and then cutting it properly.

Procedures may have changed some since I was 16, and some pizza places handle some of the process before the pizza ingredients make it to the restaurant. But back then, it took a lot of time and practice for me to learn this process and handle it properly. To this day, I still remember it takes six minutes for a large cheese pizza to cook, eight and a half minutes for a pizza with "the works" to cook, and the dough should be as close as possible to 62 degrees. The point is, I never would have realized it took so much to make a pizza unless I was shown how to do it, and I wouldn't have realized how little I did know until a horrible looking (and probably tasting) pizza came out of the oven the first time. It is the same thing with attorneys practicing in an area they have not thoroughly studied. It may look easy on the surface, but until they see the first life and estate plan in action, they won't know what kind of job they did.

While there are a lot of lawyers not able to truly handle life and estate planning for domestic partners, there are also some attorneys who understand the concepts and who are doing a good job of protecting their clients and addressing their needs. But they are still not doing the best job they could. It's the extra care and thoroughness that can give domestic partners 100 percent of all possible protection versus the 90 percent of the most important protections. Here are three typical signs your attorney may be doing a good job but not the best job possible:

To receive a free gift worth $39.97, please go to
www.estateplanningfordomesticpartners.com/gift

- They insist on drafting separate revocable trusts because of gift tax problems with having a joint trust.

- They acknowledge there are some estate tax problems but tell you only married couples can double-up their estate tax credits.

- There is no way to transfer more than $12,000 between you in any given year, so if you want to equalize your assets, one of you should just write a check for $12,000 to the other each year

Here the attorneys are showing they understand estate and gift tax implications for domestic partners, which is big step ahead of some attorneys, and they may be able to do a good job putting together a life and estate plan for you and your partner. But it also indicates they don't have some of the advanced knowledge to give you all of the protection, tax credits and joining assets together the law allows. With the right documents and language, you and your partner can combine most of your assets in a single revocable living trust. With the right revocable living trust, you and your partner can double your estate tax credits. And with the creative use of corporate entities and other techniques, it is possible to move much more than $12,000 worth of property from one partner to the other.

Finding a professional who knows how to give domestic partners the best of all possible estate planning worlds is as simple as finding them through The National Institute for Domestic Partner Estate Planning. The best documents are also easy to find since they are offered through The Estate Plan. The fact I am available to consult with these professionals on domestic partner issues and they would most likely be using the documents my firm helped develop with The Estate Plan means domestic partners have an easy way to start their search.

Of course, if you find an attorney who understands all of these issues (whether or not they work with The Estate Plan), then this book is simply here to help you work with them. Putting together your life and estate plan should not have to be a hit-or-miss proposition, and it all starts by working with the right attorney and other professionals.

Highlights of the joint revocable living trust

Because of the volume of books on the market which review the benefits of using a revocable living trust rather than a will, we will only cover the main points here. This book is more appropriately focused on applying all of the life and estate planning documents correctly to domestic partnerships. And if you start with the Partner AB-SECURE™ Trust from The Estate Plan, then all of the positive features are already incorporated into the trust. For a more detailed general description of the benefits of using a revocable living trust versus a will, I recommend reading *The Living Trust* by Henry W. Abts III.

For purposes of this chapter and domestic partnerships, the following are the main advantages of using the right revocable living trust:

1) Most property can be combined into one trust for the two of you so you are acting as one family unit.

2) Distributions upon death are all handled according to the terms of the trust, with all of the "what ifs" and contingencies in place.

3) All assets in the trust before death and those transferring into the trust automatically after death do not have to go through probate. Because the assets do not have to go through probate:

   a. settlement costs are lower

   b. settlement times are much quicker

   c. the settlement process is private.

4) The revocable living trust is much harder to contest than a last will and testament.

Again, like attorneys, all trusts are not created equal. To make sure you are getting the best documents available at an affordable price, we recommend you contact a financial advisor or attorney affiliated with The Estate Plan for a Partner AB-SECURE™ Trust (www.theestateplan.com). To find the best possible professionals available to help with these documents, you may want to search for a professional through The National Institute for Domestic Partner Estate Planning (www.NIDPestateplanning.com) and ask if he or she works with The Estate Plan.

Acting as one family unit

In setting up your joint revocable living trust, you and your partner are taking on three roles—trustors, trustees and beneficiaries. As trustors, you are the people establishing the trust. As trustees, you are both jointly empowered to utilize the trust assets for the benefit of the beneficiaries. As the beneficiaries, you are the people who enjoy the trust assets. Together you and your partner are taking control over all of the assets in the trust, together you are both running the trust for your best interests, and together you are benefiting from the trust.

In terms of owning everything together, a joint revocable living trust is as close to dual ownership as domestic partners can get without violating gift tax rules. Partners can now act upon each others' assets as if they were their own. The only difference is they are technically doing so as a trustee.

Distributions upon death

Taking into account the "estate" part of "life and estate planning," domestic partners naturally want to provide for each other when one of them passes on, but what happens when the second partner passes on? There may be children or not. There may be favorite nieces and nephews, friends or siblings. How is property divided?

All of the distribution wishes for both partners are included in the revocable living trust, listing all of the contingencies. Most domestic partner couples chose one of four main plans to start with, and then make some subtle changes. The plans are:

1. When one partner passes on, everything goes to the surviving partner outright and when he or she passes on, everything goes to beneficiaries jointly determined by both partners.

2. When one partner passes on, everything goes to the surviving partner outright and when he or she passes on, everything goes to the beneficiaries of the second partner.

3. When one partner passes on, everything is accessible to the surviving partner, and when he or she passes on, all of the first partner's separate property and one half of joint property goes to their beneficiaries, and all of the second partner's separate property and one half of joint property goes to his or her beneficiaries.

4. When one partner passes on, everything goes to the surviving partner, and when he or she passes on, everything is split in half with one half going to one partner's beneficiaries and the other half going to the other partner's beneficiaries

Let's use some examples to help make it clearer. Paul and Art are domestic partners, and they don't have any children. In putting together their joint revocable living trust, they decide they want to provide for each other. They have some different ideas to consider regarding who would receive their property after the second of them passes on. Paul has a sister Cecilia, and Art has a cousin Julio they each want to provide for.

In the first situation above, Paul and Art agree they want everything to go to each other first, and then sixty percent (60 percent) will go to Julio and forty percent (40 percent) will go to Cecilia. Regardless of how property is listed in the domestic partnership property agreement, they wish to do a 60-40 split among the two beneficiaries. This scenario is not that common except in situations where the partners have children, and in those cases, it is usually an equal division among the children.

In the second scenario above, Paul and Art wish to have everything go to the surviving partner should one of them pass on. After that, if Art was the surviving partner, then upon Art's passing, all of the property would go to Julio. If Paul was the surviving partner, then upon Paul's passing, all of the property would go to Cecilia. Because partners are usually planning together, they usually wish to jointly provide in some fashion for friends and family members together, so the "all or nothing" scenario is extremely rare.

In the third case above, Paul and Art have a domestic partnership property agreement with their trust and each has some separately accounted property and some joint property. (These domestic partnership property agreement provisions are already incorporated into The Estate Plan's Partner AB-SECURE^{TM} Trust). Because Paul's career has been much more lucrative than Art's, Paul has more assets than Art. If Paul passes on first, then all of his separate property and his one-half of the joint property will be accessible to Art during his lifetime, but the assets will still be kept accounted for separately. When Art passes on, all of Paul's separately accounted property and his one-half of the joint property will go to Cecilia. All of Art's separately controlled property and the other half of the joint property will go to Julio.

In the forth instance above, Paul and Art are leaving everything to the surviving partner when one of them passes on. Regardless of who passes on first, the survivor will be able to use everything, and then upon his passing, everything would be split evenly between Cecilia and Julio.

These are merely four of the most popular distribution methods using only one alternate beneficiary for each partner. Life is not always this simple, and there are many more contingencies for which to plan. What would happen to Cecilia's inheritance if she passed on first? If it were to go to her children equally, what if one of them passed on? Would it go to her grandchildren? At what age?

To receive a free gift worth $39.97, please go to
www.estateplanningfordomesticpartners.com/gift

A good life and estate planning attorney or advisor will press you for more and more contingencies until he or she gets into some fairly remote possibilities. If you are not throwing up your hands in frustration saying, "My God, if all of those people are dead then I just don't care anymore!" then they are not pressing you hard enough for these contingencies. Most of my clients get to the point where they don't have anyone else they wish to name, and then they are either fine with their "next of kin" getting their property, or they will leave it to a charity.

Age considerations

Another consideration in distributions is at what ages should the beneficiaries receive their inheritances? As we mentioned in the problems with simply naming young beneficiaries on accounts and life insurance, most people do not feel 18 is an appropriate age to handle a large inheritance. With the revocable living trust, you can pick ages for beneficiaries to get complete control over their inheritance.

The natural question is what are appropriate ages? I can only go by what my clients have told me over the years, but I am happy to share their wisdom with you. Most of my clients concur 25 is a good starting age, since it is about the time most people become serious about life. If they have gone through a four- year college (and done so in four years), they have had a few years to settle into a job or graduate school. And if they have gotten involved in a nightclub scene, then they have probably gotten the going-to-the-club-five- nights-a-week syndrome out of their system. That may be a good age to consider giving them control over some or all of their inheritance.

The other age my clients usually come up with is 40. If the beneficiary has not gotten their act together by the time they are 40, they are probably not going to, so there is no sense in holding the inheritance back any longer.

To receive a free gift worth $39.97, please go to
www.estateplanningfordomesticpartners.com/gift

For most of my clients, they chose one or more ages between 25 and 40 for their beneficiaries to receive their inheritance. A popular scenario is allowing them to have one-third at 25 and the rest at 30. Of course, you and your partner can choose any ages you want, and you can even choose different ages for different people.

As a final note on beneficiary ages, this does not mean the beneficiaries will not be able to have funds before they reach those ages. The ages you choose are ages when they must have absolute and complete control over the assets. Until that time, the people you have listed as trustees will be able to manage the assets and spend money on their behalf. The trustee will be left with the discretion to pay for tuition to a college or trade school, but the trustee can decline to pay for training to become a professional skateboarder. He or she can agree to pay the rent for a one-bedroom apartment with trust funds, but can decline to pay for a 10-bedroom mansion.

Benefits of avoiding probate

There are a few extraordinarily important benefits of the revocable living trust directly related to avoiding probate. Because assets in a revocable living trust avoid probate, there are lower settlement costs, shorter settlement times and private distributions.

This is also a good place to talk about exactly why trust assets avoid probate. There are many attorneys and advisors who will tell you revocable living trusts avoid probate, but rarely will they tell you how it works. Well here's the big secret:

- Probate is nothing more than an elaborate process that re-titles assets.

- Probate takes assets that remain in the name of a person even after they have died and then distributes them to the proper beneficiaries.

To receive a free gift worth $39.97, please go to
www.estateplanningfordomesticpartners.com/gift

- If nothing remains titled in the name of a deceased person, then there is no need for probate.

- When assets are titled in the name of the trust rather than an individual, when that person passes on, there is nothing to probate.

That's it. It's really that simple. Whenever assets are in a trust, they are technically in the name of the trust and not the deceased person. Because the trust assets are not in the name of the deceased person, there is no probate. Now that you know how assets in the revocable living trust avoid probate, we can briefly cover some the benefits of avoiding probate.

No probate means shorter settlement times. With the exception of shorter processes that some states allow for tiny estates, probate is a long, drawn out process. It is common for probate to take somewhere between nine months and two years to settle, and some estates drag on for considerably longer periods of time. For example, Elvis' probate started on December 20, 1977 when the will was admitted to the court, and it lasted through August 22, 1989 when the file was finally closed. While it is not likely your partner would have to wait 12 years for your assets to be available, there is no need to take any chances.

Avoiding probate also means avoiding extensive costs for appraisals, attorney fees and related costs of filling out unnecessary paperwork. While studies have varied on the exact costs, and it is different from state to state and jurisdiction to jurisdiction, the broad range costs may be between 4 percent and 10 percent of the estate assets. That can add up to some significant costs, which are not at all necessary.

Here are some estate values and corresponding estimated costs:

Estate Value	Estimated Costs
$100,000	$4,000-$10,000
$500,000	$20,000-$50,000
$1,000,000	$40,000-$100,000
$1,500,000	$60,000-$150,000
$2,000,000	$80,000-$200,000

At the time of this writing, some of the most comprehensive domestic partner life and estate plans can be created for less than $5,000, and chances are, if the costs are higher, it is because tax planning is involved. By the time both partners' estates are settled through the probate process, the costs above are doubled to account for two probates. Just in terms of cost savings, the trust is a better bet for all couples and even individuals, and considering all of the other benefits, it is a must for domestic partners.

Avoiding probate also means the settlement of your estate is private. In many states, probate court is like any other court where the filings are public documents. This means anyone can come off the street, see what assets you had when you died, who they are going to, and what that address is. Aside from the usual concerns of marketers, identity thieves and con artists seeing what accounts you had and the fact your partner is receiving them, many people feel it is simply no one's business. They're right.

I was once speaking with a financial advisor who provides workshops on revocable living trusts, and she always goes to the courthouse the morning before her workshop and gets copies of inventories for an estate that went through probate. At the workshop, she starts listing all of the personal information for the deceased person, the accounts and account balances on the date of death, and the names, addresses and dates of birth of all of the beneficiaries. During one of these workshops a man in the back row started screaming he knew the deceased woman and the presenter had no right to invade the privacy of her family like this. Well, that was exactly the point. She had every right to get the information because probate documents are public records. If you want to keep information private, then it should not go through probate.

By far, these three benefits in avoiding probate would be worth the cost and effort in establishing a revocable living trust. But there is even one more critical problem some domestic partners have that the revocable living trust can help solve.

Living trusts are more difficult to contest than wills

As mentioned earlier, it is statistically much more difficult to contest a revocable living trust than it is to contest a last will and testament. For many domestic partner couples, there is at least one family member they are at least a little concerned would create trouble. In some cases, there is outright hostility from at least one partner's family. Avoiding these conflicts usually tops the list for domestic partner life and estate planning priorities, so this is one more big benefit a revocable living trust has over a will.

Summary

The right revocable living trust can provide the means for domestic partners to bring their property together and manage it as one family unit, upon death distribute property to the people they chose, and provide age and other restrictions. Properly drafted, executed and funded revocable living trusts also can avoid all of the negatives of probate, including high costs, long settlement times, susceptibility to challenges and loss of privacy. By using the right revocable living trust as the base of their life and estate planning, domestic partners can achieve many of their goals.

Chapter Six:
Choosing the Right Trustees

While the right revocable living trust can help domestic partners reach their life and estate planning goals, it is critical to choose the right people to carry out your wishes if you become incapacitated or pass on.

Identifying the right trustees

As the two initial trustees, domestic partners really do not have to do much once their trust is established and funded. Being a trustee means you can both utilize each other's trust assets as a family, gain protection should one of you fall ill and have a distribution plan in place once you both have passed on.

The duties of your successor trustees are not quite so easy. A successor trustee has the responsibility to take care of your trust assets if you and your partner fall ill, handle all of your debts and taxes when you pass on, and possibly hold and invest assets for underage beneficiaries. While handling settlement of the trust is certainly not as difficult as taking it through probate, it can still be a long-term commitment if assets have to be handled over a period of years for younger beneficiaries.

Considering the responsibilities of your successor trustee, he or she should be chosen carefully. Fortunately, if you have already spent the time choosing your power of attorney agents, you probably already have your successor agents lined up. The criteria we recommend for choosing power of attorney agents are the same for choosing successor trustees:

- a person both partners trust with their assets and life

- financially knowledgeable but not necessarily an accountant or financial advisor

- knows when it is time to get financial help, and not someone who would be stubborn, insisting he or she can handle things, and then let your finances fall into a mess.

These three simple qualifications will hopefully guide domestic partners (and everyone else) in finding the right people to take on the role of a trustee. However simple the qualifications may seem, a lot of my clients have found it is much more difficult to actually find the people they need. And choosing from among your closest relatives may not give you the best list of trustees.

Trust

More than people will admit, at some point in their life they have seen someone's last wishes go unfulfilled because the wrong person was put in charge. An aunt wanted her house to stay in the family, but her brother sold it at an auction. A grandfather's personal effects were to be looked through by the grandchildren, but the daughter decided who got what and no one had any choice. A mother was supposed to leave a piece of land in the mountains to her daughter, but Uncle Frank sold it to a developer.

While a lot of these things may happen if the estate planning documents are vague or inadequate (or what the person *said* while alive is not what the person *wrote* in the documents), sometimes these things happen because the person in charge chooses not to go along with the orders given. That is why trust is probably the most important element in choosing a trustee.

I have found one simple question clears up a lot of confusion in identifying people to trust: "Deep down, do you believe the person would do what you ask rather than do what he or she wants?" If you believe the person would do what he or she thought was best rather than what was written in the trust, then the person should not make the list. If you believe the person would do what made the people you leave behind happy rather than follow through with your orders, then he or she should not be a trustee. Just asking this one simple question tends to greatly shorten the list of potential trustees, but it leaves the people you can truly trust on the list.

Financially knowledgeable

It is also important to have someone financially knowledgeable who can handle the duties of a trustee. However, it is not necessary for the trustee to be a financial genius. At a minimum, trustees should be able to read and understand financial statements, be able to balance a checkbook, and work with financial professionals. They certainly do not have to *be* a financial professional.

While this criteria invariably makes my clients ask if their accountant or financial advisor should be the trustee, the answer is probably "no" unless they are also close friends or family members. The true intention of the second criterion is to make sure someone who cannot balance a checkbook or someone who is a compulsive spender is not chosen as a trustee. And so, unless you know or suspect they would not exercise good judgment in reviewing and choosing investments, or they would spend money foolishly, then they might be OK to leave on the list.

Willing to seek financial help

The main duty of a trustee is to follow through on the wishes spelled out in the trust, and in some cases to manage money and assets for underage beneficiaries. Having a trustee who is stubborn and who will continue to dig himself into a hole after making a few bad decisions is not the right choice for trustee.

One of the most misunderstood aspects of trustee responsibilities is they do not have to "do everything" listed in the trust. Trustees are given a lot of power and authority, but, if they are doing their job properly, they will hire people to help execute their duties. It is not necessary to make an accountant your trustee, but the trustee should hire an accountant to handle tax returns. While it is not necessary to have a financial advisor as your trustee, if investments are going to be handled long-term, the trustee should be working with a financial advisor to make sure the trust assets are properly invested.

In choosing a trustee, you should be able to envision the trustee managing the trust assets long-term for an underage beneficiary by having a team of financial, accounting and possibly legal professionals doing their jobs and the trustee only overseeing big picture decisions. If you can only see the potential trustees pouring over financial statements and doing the taxes themselves, or you can only see them micromanaging the accountant and financial advisor, then you might want to look at other options.

Trust companies as successor trustees

Sometimes, and more often with domestic partners, there are either only one or two people whom both partners believe will make good trustees, or there is no one who fits the appropriate criteria. In these cases, it makes sense to look at trust companies as an alternative to individuals.

By no means am I saying to put trust companies as the first choice. It is always best to have an individual you trust be the trustee. They can always choose professionals to help with most of the aspects of being trustee. But if not, then a trust company may be the best bet. But which trust company?

Independent trust companies

Independent trust companies are usually the best choice when looking outside friends and family members. In general, they are less expensive than banks, provide a wide range of services and provide more personal service than bank trust departments. However, just like attorneys and financial advisors, each trust company is different.

The important questions to ask when choosing a trust company are:

1) What is your current schedule of fees?

2) Who would be handling the case?

3) What services are required, what are optional and who determines what services are used?

4) What kinds of investments are utilized?

It would be extremely useful if I could give definitive answers you should look for to the above questions, but there are none. You have to be happy with the answers you receive to the above questions, and you have to willing to look at several companies and compare.

Of course, your financial advisor may have a few recommendations for trust companies. In terms of independent trust companies, many of my clients in North Carolina choose Trust Company of the South since it is a local company with a good reputation. There is also the Santa Fe Trust Company, which has a fantastic national reputation. Both companies are worth investigating. Another option your financial advisor may offer is a trust company he or she works with specifically.

Trust companies that operate primarily through financial advisors

Depending on the firm the financial advisor works with, he or she may already have a corporate affiliation with a trust company. Even if you trust your financial advisor, be sure to do your homework and ask the same four questions as if the recommended firm were an independent trust company. You may or may not like the answers.

In my own law practice, I have had the opportunity to work with many financial advisors, and a few of their main offices are directly associated with trust companies. In essence, they are branches of the same company, and the trust clients they get are mainly through the company's financial advisors. There are both good and bad points to this association.

Because a trust company is associated with a financial advisor, there is a strong likelihood they will work with and rely on your financial advisor when making decisions. If you have a good relationship with an understanding, insightful advisor, this may be exactly the kind of relationship you want. After all, your financial advisor would probably know a lot more about your wishes and desires than the trust company. And the trust company most likely does not start working with your assets until after you have passed on.

This relationship also has a downside in that if your financial advisor is "captive," meaning she only uses company investments and insurance, the investment options for your trust assets are extremely limited. This is one of the same problems with using a traditional bank as a trustee in that the bank would typically put the assets only into CDs or savings accounts within the bank, almost guaranteeing low interest and little growth.

The best way to resolve questions regarding an affiliated trust company is to learn to what kind of investments and insurance your financial advisor has access. If she is permitted to look outside her own company and "shop the market" on your behalf, then it is likely that the trust company will follow suit. Two affiliated trust companies I have worked with in the past are Ameriprise Trust Services^{SM}, which works with Ameriprise Financial advisors, and Edward Jones Trust Company, which works with Edward Jones financial advisors. In both cases, I have not heard of any problems, and they have access to many different financial and insurance assets.

Banks

In the past, I have counseled my clients that a bank is the last institution they want for a trustee. In general, they are overpriced, cycle quickly through customer service representatives, and invest almost exclusively in bank CDs and other "in-house" instruments. Over the past several years, however, some banks have realized their shortcomings and have transformed their trust service divisions to act more independently.

While I still hesitate to recommend using a bank as a trustee for the same reasons, more and more exceptions are springing up over time. The fact is traditional bank trust departments that do not provide independent financial and trustee services on par with trust companies will lose that business. Before considering whether or not to use a bank as trustee, be sure to investigate their current fee schedule, how their trust cases are assigned and the spectrum of investments used.

Lawyers and other professionals

A final option is to name an attorney or another professional. In many cases, this ends up being an absolute last resort, because all of the other non-family and friend options are companies that presumably would last in perpetuity. (Of course, if you are naming someone because he or she is your sibling or a friend and happen to be an attorney, then it is an entirely different matter). Naming an attorney you only know professionally is almost always a bad idea because he will typically charge legal fees and trustee fees, and there would additionally be fees associated with the investment company he or she uses. While there are times legal advice is needed on behalf of a trust, a properly drafted trust will always allow the trustee to hire an attorney.

When I review trust documents drafted by another attorney, big red flags go up when I see the attorney "wrote themselves in" as successor trustee. While not always the case, the motivation for the attorney is making a lot of money in the future as the trustee and not what is in the best interests of the clients. In North Carolina, this raises ethical questions, and at the very least the attorney should have counseled the clients that they should get separate legal advice on the pros and cons of using the attorney as a trustee. My firm provides life and estate planning, and we do it very well. We can counsel trustees on their duties and we can recommend good trust companies, but we are not going to go outside our expertise and act as a trustee just because there may be a lot of money in it for us. In short, make very sure that all other options are clearly not for you and your partner before you name an attorney or other professional.

Lining up the financial power of attorney agents with the successor trustees

In addition to taking great care in lining up your and your partner's successor trustees, it is also highly recommended you name the same people as your financial power of attorney agents. We will cover more on funding the revocable living trust in Chapter Eight, but for now we'll mention that some assets will be transferred into the name of the trust, and some assets will remain outside of the trust listing the trust as a beneficiary upon death. Let's assume our friends Vince and Will have chosen to have their successor trustees and power of attorney agents be identical. This means their first successor trustees and power of attorney agent is Grace.

How a power of attorney and successor trustee authorities work together during incapacity

If Will and Vince are in a bad car accident in May and are unable to handle their financial affairs for a few months, Grace can step in and handle all of their assets because she is both the successor trustee and power of attorney agent. Here are the assets that Will and Vince have and how they are owned:

Asset	How it is owned
Condominium in New York City	Owned by Trust
ABC Brokerage Account	Owned by Trust
IRA	Owned by Vince; Will is first beneficiary; Trust is contingent beneficiary
401K	Owned by Will; Vince is first beneficiary; Trust is contingent beneficiary
Checking Account	Owned by Trust
House in the Hamptons	Owned by Trust

In looking at Will and Vince's monthly bills (and assuming health insurance is paying for their medical bills) and the fact they are not working, Grace feels she has a few options. The house in the Hamptons is paid up, but Will and Vince are still making payments on the condominium in New York City. There is also not a lot of money in their checking account.

There are investments in their brokerage account, but they seem to be earning a high rate of return right now, and she would not necessarily like to liquidate. If she did, Grace would be able to make buy and sell orders because she is now the active trustee of Will and Vince's trust.

Grace could start taking money out of Vince's IRA and Will's 401K to pay some bills, but she does not necessarily want to trigger taxes when the money is taken out. If she did make some withdraws from either of these accounts, Grace would have to use the power of attorney since the IRA and 401K are not part of the trust.

Instead of any of these options, Grace decides to use the assets Will and Vince have to generate more money and cover the monthly expenses without having to take money out. First, Grace realizes she get a much better mortgage on the property in the Hamptons and have a much lower monthly payment than the condo in the city. She uses her authority as the trustee of the trust to take out a mortgage on the Hamptons property and guarantees the loan in the name of Will and Vince using the power of attorney. She then takes the proceeds from the Hamptons house mortgage and pays off the condominium balance with some left over, which she puts into the checking account to handle bills during the next few months.

As the trustee of the trust, Grace also decides to contract with a rental company to rent out the Hamptons house and earn some income during the summer months since it is not likely that Will and Vince will be able to enjoy it anyway. This money is used to pay off the monthly mortgage and the remainder is placed into the checking account to help pay off Will and Vince's other monthly bills.

After seeing the amount of money in Will and Vince's checking account to handle bills, Grace decides that there is too much money in the account that is not earning interest. As the trustee of the trust, she opens a new money market account that is earning some interest. She also uses her power of attorney to set up direct withdrawals from the money market account for all of Will and Vince's monthly bills, and she arranges with the rental company to have all rental profits directly deposited into the money market account. She also gets online banking with the money market account with her, Will and Vince having access so she can monitor all payments and income regularly.

Grace has now effectively used a combination of trustee powers over trust assets and her authority as a power of attorney agent to handle all of Will and Vince's monthly bills, and she even set things up so she can review accounts as often as she wishes through online banking. Grace will actually make them a big profit through the summer months because of the rental property in the Hamptons, and, although it is hoped that Will and Vince will both be back at work before the end of the year, there will probably be enough money to cover the bills until next Spring without having to take money from other accounts.

You can see how Grace effectively utilized both her authority as a power of attorney agent for some items and her authority as a trustee for others. Imagine if Grace were only the power of attorney and Ben were the successor trustee. Now both of them would have to work together, agree on a strategy, and in some cases both sign papers to cover things. Also imagine if instead of Grace, Vince chose his cousin Robert to be his power of attorney. Now Grace, Ben and Robert would all have to work together on a course of action, and unless they all agreed, it would be chaos. Because of the small possibility that a power of attorney agent and successor trustee would have to work at the same time, it simply makes it easier for them to be the same person.

To receive a free gift worth $39.97, please go to
www.estateplanningfordomesticpartners.com/gift

Chapter Seven:
The Domestic Partner Property Agreement

A critical part of having the right domestic partner revocable living trust is having a domestic partner property agreement that works with the trust. By having this agreement in place, domestic partners are able to combine their assets under one trust, but at the same time the agreement keeps the assets separate for tax purposes. (For an explanation of the gift tax, please see Chapter Nine). The Partner AB-SECURE™ Trust through The Estate Plan integrates this essential agreement directly into the trust paperwork.

Combining assets without commingling them

Now that we've gone through the revocable living trust, choosing successor trustees and all of the reasons to have a joint trust for you and your partner, I can now reveal the big, secret method for combining property without violating the gift tax rules. After all, we have been recommending the assets of both partners be placed into the name of the living trust, but if these assets are not equal, it may trigger gift taxes. I'm about to tell you how it is done.

For those readers who are domestic partners looking into life and estate planning, this is a good thing for you to know when you speak with an attorney or advisor about a joint revocable living trust. For those life and estate planning attorneys who are typically recommending separate trusts because of the gift tax rules, here is the secret to successfully taking your practice up a notch and providing joint trusts for your domestic partner clients.

To receive a free gift worth $39.97, please go to
www.estateplanningfordomesticpartners.com/gift

Most committed couples want to bring everything they have together so "what's yours is mine and what's mine is yours." However, directly mixing assets is a sure way to violate the gift tax rules we mentioned previously. A properly drafted joint revocable living trust in tandem with a domestic partnership property agreement can bring many of both partner's assets into the trust. Since both partners are trustees of the trust and both are beneficiaries of the trust, they can, with a few limitations, both utilize each other's assets.

As trustees, both partners are able to control everything in the trust. The assets will be listed in the domestic partnership property agreement depending on which partner contributed an asset. Both partners can take out money and spend it, buy and sell assets, make investment decisions for the other, and otherwise do anything their partner could do if it were still in his or her separate name with these exceptions and clarifications:

1) Whenever one partner takes an asset listed as the other partner's property in the domestic partnership property agreement, the partner is deemed to have used it in his or her capacity as a trustee.

2) It is OK to utilize the partner's assets for the good of the household, the partnership, or the partner individually.

3) It is not OK to take money from one partner's account and put it into the other partner's account without triggering the gift tax.

It is important for a domestic partnership property agreement to be incorporated into the overall estate plan to work with a joint revocable living trust for domestic partners and not just be an independent document. To leave no room for error, The Estate Plan incorporates this agreement directly into a Partner AB-SECURE™ Trust.

Example using agreement

Here's an example of how a domestic partnership property agreement works with the trust. Laverne and Shirley are partners who want to create a joint revocable living trust, and they want to put as many of their assets as they can into the trust so they can act as one family unit. They create the Laverne and Shirley Revocable Living Trust. They also have the following assets:

- condominium in Milwaukee owned by Laverne and Shirley jointly (and it was jointly purchased by them)

- townhouse in California owned by Shirley

- 40 percent ownership in the Pizza Bowl restaurant/bowling alley owned by Laverne

- $200,000 in Boo-Boo Kitty Mutual Fund owned by Shirley

- $100,000 in Big L Brokerage Fund owned by Laverne.

The condominium, townhouse, Pizza Bowl stock and both mutual funds will be transferred into the name of the trust. In the domestic partnership property agreement, the condominium in Milwaukee will be listed as joint trust assets. The townhouse in California and Boo-Boo Kitty Mutual Fund will be listed as Shirley's separately accounted property, and the Pizza Bowl stock and Big L Brokerage Fund will be listed as Laverne's separately accounted property.

Both Laverne and Shirley jointly control all of the property as trustees, but for tax purposes, the assets are accounted for as if they were still separate. In other words, Laverne will still pay dividend and capital gains taxes on her separate stock, Shirley will pay property taxes on her townhouse and dividend and capital gains taxes on her mutual fund, and both Laverne and Shirley will pay property taxes on their condominium in Milwaukee.

One note for joint property that is *not* owned 50 percent by each is that it is technically separate property. For example, if a stock fund is owned as sixty percent (60 percent) by Laverne and forty percent (40 percent) by Shirley, then the fund would be titled in the name of the trust. However, the domestic partnership property agreement would list the 60 percent ownership as the separate property of Laverne and 40 percent ownership as the separate property of Shirley. It *would not* list the account in the joint property section of the agreement.

Other provisions

In addition to keeping property accounted for separately within the joint revocable living trust, the domestic partnership property agreement also assists in the orderly dissolution of the trust if the partnership breaks up. In other words, it acts as a sort of "pre-nup" (pre-marital agreement) for domestic partners.

The standard dissolution terms are simple:

- Whatever the first partner has listed as separate property is hers to take.

- Whatever the second partner has listed as separate property is hers to take.

- All jointly owned property is divided equally between the partners.

The standard division of assets keeps separate property separate and divides joint property down the middle; this does not have to be the case. The agreement can be amended to provide a different form of asset division. However, it is important to keep in mind any unequal division may incur gift taxes if the "unequal" division exceeds $12,000 in the year of division.

While many domestic partner breakups can be handled amicably, this is not always the case. There are enough emotional difficulties associated with committed partners going separate ways, so having a guideline for dividing the property fairly and equitably can reduce the amount of stress (not to mention legal fees) in seeing the division made final.

Summary

While domestic partners typically want to combine assets as one family unit for life and estate planning purposes, a revocable living trust can offer an ideal solution. However, in order to avoid onerous gift and other tax complications, a domestic partner property agreement can account for property separately, avoid tax complications and also provide for a division of assets and dissolution of the trust in case the domestic partners break up.

Chapter Eight:
Funding the Trust

Once you have a revocable living trust in place for you and your partner, you have to make sure all of your assets work with your trust. In other words, you have to make sure your revocable living trust is funded properly. A revocable living trust will keep all of the assets in the trust from having to go through probate. Therefore, to avoid probate completely, you have to make sure all of your assets are in the trust or are set up to transfer into the trust upon death. Just having the documents is not enough.

Most of the problems people hear about revocable living trusts are just like the stories people hear about hospitals. There is nothing inherently wrong with hospitals. Hospitals and the people who work in them can save your life, help you recover and then release you from their care allowing you to have a longer or better life. But then there are the stories of medication mix-ups, surgeries happening on the wrong person or the wrong part of the body, or a host of other malpractice problems. But all of these problems stem from the practice of medicine being done poorly.

It is the same with a revocable living trust not being effective in doing what it is supposed to do—avoid probate, preserve privacy, lower costs and shorten settlement times. The main area where revocable trusts fall short is when assets are not set up properly to work in conjunction with the trust. And so the revocable living trust naysayers, who are mostly attorneys who do a lot of probate work, are way off target when they suggest people not use revocable trusts at all. What they should be saying is if you have a revocable living trust, just make sure it is drafted properly and your assets are in place to take full advantage of it. After all, no one is suggesting just because there are mistakes made in hospitals we should simply close them all down—we just need to make sure that things happen the way they are supposed to.

While each asset is a little different, there are three main kinds of changes that have to take place depending on the type of asset. If your revocable living trust was drafted properly and an "assignment of personal assets" or similar form has been used, then all of your personal assets like clothing, furniture and appliances are already in the trust. This even covers things like the food in the refrigerator and the change between the seat cushions. What we need to be concerned with are items such as real estate and timeshares, investment and retirement accounts, bank accounts and other assets that have some sort of title to them.

The first kind of change is re-titling an asset in the name of the revocable living trust. In short, you and your partner are changing these assets so technically you no longer own the asset but your joint trust does. But don't worry. You still control everything in the trust and can still do everything you normally would do as if it were property owned by both of you. The second kind of change is making the trust the primary beneficiary in case you pass on. You still remain the owner on the account, but now when you pass on it can go directly into the trust without having to go through probate to get there. The third change is to make a person the primary beneficiary and the trust becomes the contingent beneficiary. In this instance you keep control of the account, but if you pass it goes to another person, namely your partner, and not the trust. If your partner passes on before you do, then it would go to the trust to be distributed. *The most important thing is that all of these possible transfers happen without probate.*

While there may be different permutations and exceptions, these are the three main kinds of changes that need to be done. We will now go through some specifics on these changes one at a time, discuss which assets require a specific method, and then go into some exceptions, future steps and maintenance. But first, here are a few basics regardless of what kind of change is made.

The Basics

Always use the legal trust name and the legal names of people. The name of the trust is typically found in the first few pages of the revocable living trust. We also prepare a report for our clients called "Property Title and Beneficiary Changes & Designations" and list the proper name of the trust on the first page. This typically reads something like "The Revocable Living Trust of Jessica Tate and Mary Campbell." For a person's name, if their name is John Wilkes Booth or Lee Harvey Oswald, you should not refer to them as Wilkee Booth or Ossie Oswald, even though that is how people generally know them. Always use the full proper name.

One benefit of working with a financial advisor through The Estate Plan is the advisor will outline and assist with a lot of these changes for clients using the exact names and information, and will also work with an attorney for any legal documents needed to make these changes, such as drafting deeds.

Second, always look at what kind of asset or account you are handling and ask "have I paid income taxes on this yet?" This is actually a big consideration. Any account that is "tax-qualified," meaning it is for retirement and you were able to put that money away without paying income taxes on it, should never be transferred directly into the name of the trust. If you do, then IRS regulations may treat that as if you had taken all of the money out in one year, and you are subject to taxes and possibly penalties. If you are in doubt, contact your attorney or tax professional before making any such change.

Finally, start with a list of all of your accounts and assets that have some kind of title to them and make sure you go through the list until all of the changes are completed.

Re-titling assets in the name of the trust

In some cases, re-titling an asset so it is in the name of the trust is the best course of action. This is certainly the case with real estate, and is best for mutual funds, savings accounts, checking accounts, money market accounts, and other non-qualified brokerage accounts. By non-qualified, I mean that you have paid income taxes on the money before you put it into the account. As a word of caution, unless you are working with a financial advisor affiliated with The Estate Plan we encourage people to handle as many of the transfers on their own as they can to save on the costs of funding the trust. However, transferring ownership of real estate and timeshares involves preparing a legal deed to make those transfers. Drafting a deed is something only a licensed attorney should do, so if this has not been taken care of by your attorney, contact him or her.

In making changes to accounts, the type of form you would need is probably titled something like a "change of ownership" or "change of title." In any event, your financial advisor or personnel at the institution should know which form is required to change the ownership of the account in the right way. If your advisor does not know, contact your attorney and have him or her speak with the financial institution.

Changing the primary beneficiary

There are also some situations where changing the ownership is not as beneficial as changing the beneficiary. The best example is a life insurance policy. The most important part of the life insurance contract is who gets the proceeds. In this case, the trust is the right beneficiary. While it is possible to make the revocable living trust the owner, the paperwork is usually much more involved and has no added benefit. Instead, it becomes easier to keep your life insurance policy in your name and simply make your trust the primary beneficiary. Upon death, all it would take is a copy of the death certificate for the proceeds to pay into your trust.

Please also note at this point we are talking about situations that don't involve estate tax problems. If you have large life insurance policies and may be subject to estate taxes, other steps can be taken to account for ownership of life insurance while saving estate taxes through an Irrevocable Life Insurance Trust (See Chapter Twelve).

Changing the contingent beneficiary

Finally, there are a few situations where you want to keep ownership of an account, name another individual as the primary beneficiary, and then list the trust as the contingent or secondary beneficiary. In all of these cases, you are naming a spouse or partner the primary beneficiary of an IRA, 401K or other tax-qualified account for income tax purposes, and then listing your living trust as the contingent beneficiary. For married couples, there are special benefits regarding tax-qualified accounts in that the surviving spouse can do a "roll-over" when one spouse passes on, meaning placing the assets in the account into the spouse's own IRA and then take the money out when he or she chooses. In doing so, there can be some considerable tax-deferred growth, but the main catch is this is only available to spouses right now.

We also recommend this same set up be done for tax-qualified accounts for domestic partners even though they are not married. Our reason for making this recommendation is the funds are still going to the person they want, and if that person passes on first, it will still end up in the trust to be distributed to other beneficiaries when the second partner passes on. Under some new federal laws, domestic partners have the opportunity to defer income taxes when they inherit their partner's retirement account. (For more information, please download the free report at www.domesticpartneriras.com) Also, if in the future domestic partners gain the same "roll-over" option, the accounts will already be set up properly and another change will not be necessary. But until that time, there is nothing lost in still setting up the beneficiaries on the accounts this way.

Difficult items

And now, because we are not in a perfect world, there are a few items that present difficulties. First and foremost, there are automobiles. The main problem with handling automobiles, at least in North Carolina, is that auto insurance agents generally don't understand what we are doing in setting up a revocable living trust, and so they feel compelled to say your car is now a corporate vehicle, therefore the coverage is much higher and your premiums will go up. There is also no way to put a transfer upon death beneficiary designation on a car title, and therefore there is no way to have the automobiles avoid probate without creating hassles during life. But as I tell my clients, as long as your trustee has the car keys and the car is registered and insured, it really doesn't matter if it takes a few months for the car to go through probate.

The second item that creates some difficulties is CDs. And no, I don't mean the music kind. Certificates of Deposit are typically registered in the owner's name and can't be changed until the certificates become due without having substantial penalties. Therefore, the advice our firm typically gives is to wait until the CDs are due, and then if you wish to keep the proceeds invested in CDs, work with the bank to re-title them in the name of the trust at that time. Also, it may be worth checking with the bank to see if it can somehow place a beneficiary designation on the CD. Then it is probably easier to simply list the trust as the primary beneficiary.

Finally, while this is not really a difficult step in initially funding the trust, a lot of my clients have had some difficulty in refinancing a mortgage once the land is in the trust. This is not a legal difficulty or even a financial difficulty. The fact is despite the large increase in the use of revocable living trusts over the past 20 years and more, a lot of mortgage lenders still panic when they see the property is in a trust. *Don't let their panic affect you.* Typically all that is needed is a few pages of the trust faxed to the lender, or in some rare cases, a letter from the attorney. If your lender is still in a panic or requires you to transfer your property back into your name before it will refinance, then it may be time to consider another mortgage lender. If not, then one deed must be created and executed transferring the land back into your individual name, and then a second deed should be executed after the refinancing is completed in order to transfer the property back into the trust.

We have gone over all of the different kinds of transfers, the different kinds of assets, what needs to be done to each, and even reviewed some trouble areas. If everything is done properly, your revocable living trust should now be complete and well-funded. But what happens next? As you go forward in life, there will be many opportunities to open new accounts, buy and sell properties, and make transfers. Each time you have a new asset with a title or account name on it, something needs to be done to make sure it works with the trust. In these cases, simply review this program again to see what needs to be done.

As a word of caution again about mortgages, if you are buying property in the future and will have a mortgage on it, it may be more convenient, and certainly less stressful, to initially purchase the property in your own name, wait about two weeks, and then transfer the property into the name of the trust. In general, this just makes things run more smoothly.

With most situations in this book, we recommend you consult with an attorney who fully understands life and estate planning. However, with regard to funding your trust, you will receive even better help with a financial advisor who understands the same field. The Estate Plan has a nationwide network of such advisors who typically work with estate planning attorneys. As I have also mentioned, my firm is available to consult with all advisors and attorneys who are in The Estate Plan's network, and certified professionals can be found through The National Institute for Domestic Partner Estate Planning.

Summary

The right revocable living trust can provide domestic partners with many of benefits they are looking for, but the trust only works if it is properly funded. In general, assets have to be re-titled in the name of the trust, set up so the account pays into the trust upon death, or set up so the account pays out first to the partner and second to the trust.

Chapter Nine:
The Gift Tax in More Detail

We've gone through the revocable living trust, the domestic partner property agreement, and the proper funding of the trust. However much I recommend domestic partners utilize the right revocable living trust, I still have some clients who are somehow not convinced gift taxes are "real" or if they are, then it does not apply to them. "After all, we have friends who just used joint property, and nothing has happened to them." The answer I give them is, "nothing has happened to them *yet*."

I also hear some partners complain they wish to be able to say 100 percent that their property is owned together and a separate property agreement seems to fly in the face of that intent. Unfortunately, it is a necessary part of the agreement to avoid the gift tax rules in place. Don't let this one piece of paperwork hold up a good life and estate plan, and don't leave out this document and potentially expose huge gift taxes. If you were sufficiently convinced you and your partner needed a joint revocable living trust with a domestic partnership property agreement, you can proceed to the next chapter. If you still need some convincing or you would like to see the numbers in action, then please read the following two examples:

Example 1 of gift taxes without domestic partnership property agreement

Ellen and Anne have decided to put together a life and estate plan through an attorney who works with The Estate Plan. They go through all of the proper documents, enacting a Partner AB-SECURE™ Trust, healthcare powers of attorney, financial powers of attorney, living wills, nomination of conservator documents, and others, including the integrated domestic partnership property agreement in the trust. All of the documents have been properly drafted and executed, and Ellen and Anne even handled all of the funding with their financial advisor.

Because Ellen came to the relationship with more assets than Anne, she had considerably more assets listed on her separate part of the domestic partnership property agreement than Anne did. Here is how the trust assets were listed along with their current values:

Asset	Listed in Agreement	Value
Home in Beverly Hills	Ellen	$2,000,000
Dance, Dance, Dance Co.	Ellen	$1,000,000
ABC Mutual Fund	Ellen	$1,000,000
Vermont Townhouse	Anne	$100,000
NBC Mutual Fund	Anne	$100,000
Condominium in NYC	Anne and Ellen	$400,000

After all of the paperwork is completed and Anne and Ellen have an excellent, functioning life and estate plan, Ellen and Anne start talking about the domestic partnership property agreement. They don't like the fact their assets are still listed separately, and they want to have everything truly mixed as 50-50 ownership. Without consulting their attorney or financial advisor, they decide to revoke the agreement.

Revoking the agreement just cost Ellen $341,120 in taxes. Ellen also just lost all but $1,000,000 of her estate tax credits, so now when she passes on every single penny past $1,012,000 will be taxed. Furthermore, Anne just lost $38,000 of her $1 million lifetime gift exemption, and she can pass on $1,912,000 at death without estate taxes. If Ellen passes on first, there will be a lot of estate taxes, but the fact is there will be a lot of estate taxes paid when the second partner passes on regardless of who goes first.

That's outrageous! How can this be? All Ellen and Anne did was cancel an agreement!

Well, what Ellen and Anne actually did by revoking the agreement was allow all of the property they titled in the name of the trust to be considered owned by them equally. And that is actually what they wanted to have happen. And so each partner made a gift to the other partner as follows:

- Ellen gave half of the value of the mansion to Anne, which is a $1,000,000 gift.

- Ellen gave half of the value of the Dance, Dance, Dance Co. stock to Anne, which is a $500,000 gift.

- Ellen gave half of the value of the ABC Mutual Fund stock to Anne, which is a $500,000 gift.

- Anne gave half of the value of the Vermont townhouse to Ellen, which is a $50,000 gift.

- Anne gave half of the value of the NBC Mutual fund to Ellen, which is a $50,000 gift.

To receive a free gift worth $39.97, please go to
www.estateplanningfordomesticpartners.com/gift

- The condominium in New York City was already paid for jointly by both Ellen and Anne, and therefore there is no change.

Ellen's gifts to Anne total $2 million, only $12,000 of which is exempt from gift taxes. Anne's gifts to Ellen total $100,000, only $12,000 of which is exempt from gift taxes. Because each can only give $1 million in gifts during life, Ellen will have to pay $341,120 in taxes now because she went well beyond that amount.

Example 2 of gift taxes without domestic partnership property agreement

Carlos and Dave are committed domestic partners, and, based on the advice they got from their cable guy Larry, decide to put all of their assets into joint tenancy. This means all of Carlos' previously separate accounts now have Dave listed as an owner and vice versa. Carlos has only a house worth $500,000 and Dave has a mutual fund worth $500,000. After they put each other's name on the title to the house and the mutual fund, they decide to talk to their accountant.

The accountant gave them the bad news: Carlos actually gave a gift of $250,000 to Dave, the first $12,000 of which is exempt, leaving a taxable gift of $238,000 from Carlos to Dave. Assuming Carlos started with the whole $1,000,000 in lifetime federal gift tax credits, we subtract the $238,000 from the $1,000,000 leaving $762,000 that can be gifted in the future (beyond the $12,000 annual exclusion), and only $1,762,000 that can passed from Carlos to Dave, or anyone else for that matter, without estate taxes. The same is now also true of the gifts given from Dave to Carlos.

For many people, that may not sound so terrible, but imagine if Dave and Carlos did not go to their accountant and fill out the proper gift tax forms. That's when you usually hear two of the IRS' favorite words—"interest" and "penalties."

There is also a huge potential *state* gift tax problem, depending on the state in which the partners reside. For example, in North Carolina with Carlos and Dave being "Class C Beneficiaries" to each other (since they are not married) each dollar over $12,000 is an immediately taxable gift. This would have actually resulted in an immediate tax of $26,710 due from Carlos and the same from Dave. A total of $53,420 in taxes would have to be paid, out of pocket and right away, as a result of re-titling these two accounts. (I wonder if the cable guy Larry has legal malpractice insurance.)

Summary

As you can see, federal and state gift taxes can create substantial problems for domestic partners if property is not combined appropriately. Joint property may sound like a simpler solution, but it can have devastating consequences. Using a joint revocable living trust with a domestic partnership property agreement with the right professionals can help alleviate or avoid these problems.

SECTION III:
ADVANCED ESTATE TAX-SAVINGS TECHNIQUES

The first two sections of this book are essential reading for all committed domestic partner couples. The third section truly moves to the next level, and it is primarily written for those domestic partners who may potentially have estate taxes as well as attorneys and other professionals who wish to learn more about helping their domestic partner clients avoid them.

If you are not sure if you and your partner have potential estate tax problems, please download the free Excel spreadsheet by going to www.estateplanningfordomesticpartners.com/spreadsheet. If you and your partner do not have any potential estate tax issues, or if such issues would be adequately handled by a Partner AB-SECURE™ Trust through The Estate Plan, then we hope you will at least find Section III of interest.

Chapter Ten:
Introduction to the Estate Tax

One of the highest taxes imposed by the U.S. government is an estate tax on larger estates. Fortunately for married couples, there are some tax breaks. Unfortunately for domestic partners, these same tax breaks are not automatically available as they are with married couples. But not all hope is lost. This section contains some advanced techniques domestic partners can use to claim many of the same breaks married couples have.

Before going into how domestic partners can cure or reduce potential estate taxes, it is important to understand exactly what the tax is and how it works.

Lifetime estate tax credits

Each U.S. citizen has a lifetime bank of estate tax exemptions, which can be applied towards estate taxes upon death. The legislation currently in effect has these exemptions changing over time depending on the year of death. The exemptions are:

- 2007-2008 the exemption is $2,000,000

- 2009 the exemption is $3,500,000

- 2010 there are no estate taxes

- 2011 the current law expires making the exemption revert to $1,000,000

Yes, this sounds ridiculous, but that's Congress for you. For planning purposes, our office uses the $1,000,000 amount since most of our clients plan to be around past 2011. What this means is that when a person passes on, he or she can distribute up to $1,000,000 in property to anyone, at its fair market value, without estate taxes. Anything above $1,000,000 is taxed starting at 41 percent.

For example, let's assume that Stan and Kyle each have $1 million in assets, and they want to leave everything to each other. When the second of them passes on, they want to leave everything equally to Stan's nephew Kenny and Kyle's nephew Eric. Assuming no growth, if Stan passes on first, then Kyle has $2 million in assets. When Kyle passes on, again assuming no growth, then there is one $2 million estate, and Kyle's estate has to pay $435,000 in estate taxes, leaving Kenny and Eric with $782,500 each rather than $1 million each.

Here's how the tax is computed. First, you compute the total amount of the estate. For further information, see the IRS instructions for completing form 706. Using the federal tables found in Table A of that form, on page 4 of the instructions as of this printing, you see for a $2 million estate, the tax is exactly $780,800. You get this number by looking at the amounts in columns A and B, seeing what the tax is for the amount in column B, and then multiplying any "excess" over the amount in column B by the percentage in column D. Yes, this sounds complicated, but we will look at Kyle and Stan's example first and then at a more illustrative example afterwards.

Also, please note while professionals say "the first $1 million is estate tax free," that is not entirely accurate. What you get instead is $345,800 in tax credits, which means if your estate were exactly $1 million, then there would be no estate taxes. In the example of Kyle's estate, by subtracting $345,800 in credits from the $780,800 tax on a $2 million estate, you see the taxes are actually $435,000. (If you first "took off" the first $1 million and looked at the tables, the result would be $345,800 in taxes, which is not accurate—the number is off by $89,200.)

Let's also compute another estate of $1,750,000 to better illustrate how the table works. First, the amount of the estate is between $1,500,000 (Column A) and $2 million (Column B). The tax on the $1,500,000 is $555,800. There is also an "extra" $250,000, which is the amount over $1,500,000 we have for this estate ($1,750,000 minus $1,500,000=$250,000). We multiply the additional $250,000 by the percentage in Column D, which is 45 percent, and that comes out to $112,500. Add $112,500 to the original $555,800, and we have a preliminary tax of $668,300. From there, we can subtract the estate tax credits of $345,800 from the amount of the tax and arrive at a tax of $322,500. ($668,300 - $345,800 = $322,500).

Now that we have done the math, let's see how we can save some money on taxes. We'll start with married couples.

Credit shelter trust

Whenever the government allows added estate tax breaks, there are usually some strings attached. For example, whenever an estate gives money to a charity, it can deduct the value of the gift from the taxable estate. In other words, you have to give up the asset in order to have it deducted from the taxable estate. (How generous of the IRS!)

This give-and-take also applies with smaller restrictions for a credit shelter trust for married couples. Whenever one spouse passes on and both of the spouses are U.S. citizens, the surviving spouse can inherit an unlimited amount of property without any estate taxes. The problem comes when the second spouse passes on and he or she only has the $2 million in estate tax credits. By having a credit shelter trust, the deceased spouse, prior to passing on, could have placed assets in the credit shelter trust so that when the second spouse passes on, they have effectively "doubled up" their credits. Again, with a $4 million combined estate, this can save the next generation up to $920,000 in estate taxes.

In order to save on the estate taxes, the surviving spouse has to give up a few things. Considering the amounts of money we are talking about and the way assets can be arranged, the financial flexibility given up is not too great. The surviving spouse is allowed to:

- receive all income generated from the credit shelter trust

- use any property in the trust

- receive 5 percent or $5,000 as a trustee's fee for managing the trust

- sell, exchange, or buy assets in and out of the trust.

Each of these rules represents the maximum powers the surviving spouse can have, and in order to receive the second two benefits, the surviving spouse must be a trustee of the credit shelter trust. Of course, a good financial advisor becomes imperative in allocating assets so it can generate no income, a little income, or a lot of income depending on the needs of the surviving spouse.

But a credit shelter trust is not available to domestic partners. However, the "SECURE™" part of the Partner AB-SECURE™ Trust can provide the additional estate tax credits. We will explore this tax-savings feature in the next chapter.

Chapter Eleven:
The SECURE™ Trust – a credit shelter trust for non-spouses

In the previous chapter we reviewed the federal estate tax and the lifetime estate tax credits each individual has. There is within the law a special tax trust married couples can take advantage of called a credit shelter trust. When the second spouse passes on, there is a way to "double up" the tax credits. When a married couple uses a credit shelter trust (in 2011 and beyond), the couple can pass on up to $2 million without estate taxes (instead of just $1 million).

While the special credit shelter trust is only available to married couples, our firm in conjunction with The Estate Plan has developed a new trust that can give the same estate tax breaks for only a few more restrictions. The SECURE™ (Special Estate Credit Retention) part of the Partner AB-SECURE™ Trust, can hold the assets of the first partner to pass on, have them available for the surviving partner through an independent trustee, and then when the second partner passes on, both estates will have had their estate tax credits applied. (Please keep in mind we are only discussing federal estate taxes. State estate taxes vary, and if you have specific questions you should contact a tax professional in your area.) The best way to explain how this works is to use an example:

Example

George and Neil are partners and have accumulated quite a bit in assets. They naturally want to provide for each other, and then leave their assets to Neil's nieces Barbara and Jenna. Together they have a joint revocable living trust, and for the sake of keeping this simple, let's assume that George has $1 million in oil company stock as his separately accounted for property, and Neil has $1 million in separately account property mixed among real estate holding, voting machine stocks and cash.

If George passes on leaving everything to Neil without a SECURE™ Trust in 2011, and then Neil passes on a year later in 2012, here is how the estate taxes would look:

1) George leaves his $1 million to Neil; no federal estate taxes.

2) Neil leaves a $2 million estate, resulting in $435,000 in estate taxes.

3) The $1,565,000 remaining goes to Jenna and Barbara.

Now let's use the same facts but having George and Neil utilize a SECURE™ Trust instead:

1) George leaves his $1 million to Neil through their joint Partner AB-SECURE™ Trust, and Neil allocates George's $1 million to the "SECURE™" portion of the trust, so an independent trustee can manage the assets for Neil for the remainder of his life and then pass the remainder onto Jenna and Barbara when Neil passes on. There are no estate taxes.

2) Neil passes on leaving his own $1 million estate. Neil technically never has control over George's SECURE™ Trust assets, so they are not counted as part of his taxable estate.

3) Neil's $1 million goes to Jenna and Barbara with no federal estate taxes. George's SECURE™ Trust $1 million in assets goes to Jenna and Barbara with no federal estate taxes. *These estates through use of a SECURE™ Trust managed to avoid $435,000 in estate taxes.*

Restrictions on credit shelter trust vs. SECURE™ Trust

In the previous chapter, we reviewed the restrictions on a credit shelter trust. The surviving spouse has some access to the trust, usually in conjunction with an independent trustee, but there are some restrictions. The most access a surviving spouse can have is:

- The surviving spouse can receive all of the income generated by the trust.

- The surviving spouse can use any property in the trust, such as house or vehicles.

- If the surviving spouse is a trustee, then he or she can be paid 5 percent or $5,000 each year, whichever is greater, for being the trustee.

- If the surviving spouse is a trustee, then he or she can buy, sell and exchange property within the trust.

As long as these restrictions or greater ones are imposed on the surviving spouse, up to the full $1 million in estate tax credits (post-2011) can be applied to the trust assets when the first spouse passes on. In order for domestic partners to get the same estate tax breaks with a SECURE™ Trust, there are some greater restrictions needed.

- The surviving partner can receive all of the income generated by the trust.

- The surviving partner can use property in the trust, such as houses or vehicles.

- The surviving partner cannot be a trustee, and therefore an independent trustee must make decisions regarding whether or not to distribute assets to the surviving partner.

While this may seem like a lot to give up in order to get the estate tax credits, and in strict legal terms it is only control being given up. It is recommended a close friend or family member who is not going to eventually inherit property from the SECURE™ Trust be the trustee. In practical terms, the trustee will probably give the person anything he or she wanted. But there are also some practical terms written into the trust which will make things easier for the surviving partner.

It is specifically recommended that the trustee work with the surviving partner to purchase real estate and other hard assets the partner can use rather than putting money into securities and other assets. This may involve the SECURE™ Trust portion purchasing the surviving partner's interest in the family home. Now the surviving partner can live in the house, and can invest the proceeds in whatever desired. It makes life easier for the surviving partner because he or she does not need to go to the trustee in order to get money.

Example

Let's use an example. Suppose Norm and Cliff are partners with a revocable living trust and domestic partnership property agreement. Norm passes on. He leaves all of his assets through the SECURE™ Trust for Cliff, which includes a one-half interest in their home in Boston worth $250,000 (for his half), his stock in Cheers Brewing Company worth $500,000, and a half interest in a house in Cape Cod worth $250,000 (for his half). Cliff owns the other half interest in the home in Boston worth $250,000 (for his half), the other half interest in the home in Cape Cod worth $250,000 (for his half), and $500,000 in UPS stock.

Norm directed all of his assets be placed into the SECURE™ Trust, and now to make things as convenient as possible for Cliff, the trustee, Sam, arranges to exchange the $500,000 in Cheers Brewing Company stock for Cliff's $500,000 interest in the Boston and Cape Cod properties. Cliff retains the ability to live in and use both properties, but now he has investments worth $1 million he can access without having to go to Sam. (There are most likely some capital gains taxes involved in these transfers, so please consult a CPA or other tax professional if you wish to run different tax scenarios for you and your partner in making these exchanges. While no one but the government is happy with the capital gains taxes that might be incurred here, it is certainly less than $435,000 in estate taxes that would have resulted from not using the SECURE™ Trust at all).

Tax savings for the next generation

To illustrate the potential estate tax savings power of the SECURE™ Trust, we are going to run through some scenarios comparing estates with and without the SECURE™ Trust assets.

Scenario 1

Janet and Crissy are domestic partners, and both partners own equal amounts of assets through their revocable living trust with domestic partner property agreement. Crissy has $700,000 in assets and so does Janet. Janet passes on in 2012 leaving her $700,000 to Crissy through their revocable living trust. Because Janet's estate is less than $1,000,000, there are no federal estate taxes. Crissy passes on two years later, leaving her and Janet's siblings their assets. Assuming there was no growth in assets, Crissy's estate does have estate taxes on the $400,000 "extra" to the tune of $167,000.

If instead Crissy and Janet utilized SECURE™ Trust provisions in the Partner AB-SECURE™ Trust, the tax scenario would be much different. Janet passes on in 2012 leaving all of her $700,000 in assets to the SECURE™ Trust, so now Crissy will be able to work with Jack, the trustee. The assets are used for Crissy's benefit but are technically not her property. There are no estate taxes when Janet passes on because her estate was less than $1 million. When Crissy passes on in 2014, she leaves her $700,000 in assets through the revocable trust to her and Janet's siblings. Because her estate was less than $1 million, there are no estate taxes. Now that Crissy has passed on, Jack can release the assets in the

SECURE™ Trust portion to Janet and Crissy's siblings, also without estate taxes. Having the SECURE™ Trust provisions utilized saved Janet and Crissy's siblings $167,000 in estate taxes.

Scenario 2

Let's suppose that Janet and Crissy have more assets, but they are still essentially equal in what is accounted for in their names through the Partner AB-SECURE™ Trust with an integrated domestic partnership property agreement. Janet and Crissy each have $1,200,000. Janet passes on in 2012 leaving everything to Crissy, and then Crissy passes on in 2014 leaving everything to her and Janet's siblings.

Suppose there were no trust and no SECURE™ Trust provisions. When Janet passes on in 2012, she will have a taxable estate of $1,200,000, incurring taxes of $82,000. The remaining amount of $1,118,000 goes to Crissy. When Crissy passes on in 2014, she has a combined estate of $2,318,000, only applying the estate tax credits for the first $1,000,000. The tax bill comes to $584,460, and the remaining $1,733,540 will go to Crissy and Janet's siblings. In all, Crissy and Janet lost $666,460 to estate taxes.

If Crissy and Janet used the SECURE™ Trust provisions, the tax situation would be much different. When Janet passes on in 2012, she puts her assets in the SECURE™ Trust but still has estate taxes of $82,000, leaving $1,118,000 to go into the trust. When Crissy passes on in 2014, she would also have $82,000 in estate taxes. The remainder of her assets will go to her and Janet's siblings ($1,118,000), the amounts in the SECURE™ Trust will also go to their siblings ($1,118,000), and the total tax bill will be only $164,000. In all, the SECURE™ Trust saved $502,460.

Scenario 3

So far, we've only looked at equal estates. Let's use our final example to illustrate uneven estates. Let's assume Janet has $2.5 million and Crissy has no assets of her own. If Janet passes on in 2012, leaving everything to Crissy through their revocable living trust with domestic partnership property agreement, there would be taxes in the amount of $670,000. If Crissy then passed on in 2014, there would be taxes on the entire remaining amount of $1,830,000 totaling $358,500, leaving only $1,471,500 to Crissy and Janet's siblings. That's a lot of estate taxes ($1,028,500), and to be charged twice does not really seem fair… but that's the way it is.

If Janet and Crissy used the SECURE™ Trust provisions, Janet's estate could pay the estate taxes of $670,000, leave $1 million to Crissy in the revocable living trust, and place the remainder of her assets ($830,000) into the SECURE™ Trust. When Crissy passes on, she will have no estate taxes on her $1 million, and there are no further estate taxes on the assets in the SECURE™ Trust. In all, the SECURE™ Trust saved Janet and Crissy's siblings $358,500 in taxes.

Exclusivity of SECURE™ Trust

In addition to providing potential estate tax savings in the hundreds of thousands of dollars for domestic partners, these tax-saving features are also available in a flexible manner. The default set up of the Partner AB-SECURE™ Trust allocates everything to the surviving partner through the "B" part of the trust, which is fully accessible to the surviving partner but has no future estate tax savings. The surviving partner has to sign off on property going to the SECURE™ Trust using something called a "disclaimer." (This form is provided with all Partner AB-SECURE™ Trusts).

To receive a free gift worth $39.97, please go to
www.estateplanningfordomesticpartners.com/gift

The SECURE™ Trust was developed by The Law Offices of Jeffrey G. Marsocci, PLLC, and remains exclusive through our firm and through The Estate Plan only. If you and your partner have sufficient assets that make estate tax planning necessary, contact our firm at (919) 844-7993. Other professionals who understand domestic partner planning can be reached through The National Institute for Domestic Partner Estate Planning at www.NIDPestateplanning.com. If you prefer, you can also contact The Estate Plan directly at 1 (800) 350-1234.

Chapter Twelve:
Irrevocable Life Insurance Trusts

Most Americans have life insurance of some kind, whether it is a $5,000 policy through work to help with final expenses, or separately purchased policies totaling millions of dollars. Domestic partners are no exception. One widespread belief fostered by the insurance industry is there are no taxes on life insurance. "That is phenomenal!" you may be saying. "So all I have to do to pass large amounts of money without any taxes is to have a large life insurance policy!"

While this makes for a great selling point in the insurance industry, it is just not true. The beneficiary of a life insurance policy does not pay *income* taxes on the money received, but the deceased person's estate must pay *estate* taxes on the full value of the life insurance policy. So while insurance agents are raking in hefty commissions on oversized insurance policies, their clients' estates are stuck paying huge estate tax bills… unless their insurance agent was actually a qualified financial advisor who works with attorneys to avoid those taxes through an irrevocable life insurance trust.

Let me be clear about my personal prejudices about the life insurance industry and explain them. I have little respect for "life insurance agents" (as I will refer to them) who in my eyes are somewhere on the same rung as the stereotypical used car salesmen who will do anything to sell you the most expensive car they can. These agents are only out to make as much money as they can by selling you the highest priced "product" they can.

There are also "financial advisors" (as I will call them) for whom I have a lot of respect. Financial advisors will review your total financial situation and present a comprehensive plan including investments, savings and possibly one or more life insurance policies. They also primarily want to assist you with your overall financial picture for the rest of your life and provide security for your family rather than just make a sale and move on. I have yet to hear from a client that their *life insurance agent* suggested an irrevocable life insurance trust, but I frequently hear from clients who say their *financial advisor* recommended one.

So what exactly is an irrevocable life insurance trust? The concept is simple when examined, but creating and maintaining one is something that should not be done without the assistance of a qualified estate planning attorney and financial advisor working together. In short, an irrevocable life insurance trust, or ILIT for short, is a permanent trust with an independent trustee that owns a life insurance policy on your life. By giving over complete control to your life insurance policy to the trustee, giving ownership of the policy to your trust, and having the proceeds of the life insurance policy pay into the trust, the proceeds are not counted as part of your taxable estate.

Since I have been recommending documents from The Estate Plan, it is worth mentioning they also provide those kinds of documents through the attorneys within their network. However, The Estate Plan calls these documents "preservation trusts." There is no difference between an ILIT and a Preservation Trust except for the name. For purposes of this book and chapter, I will refer to them as ILITs since that is the term with which most clients, financial professionals and attorneys are accustomed.

There are several aspects of an ILIT to be examined in detail before you and your partner look into them. While an ILIT is a great tool for avoiding unnecessary estate taxes, you should be well informed of what you are giving up to get those tax benefits.

An ILIT is irrevocable

As the name implies, an irrevocable life insurance trust is… well… irrevocable. Once it is set up, it cannot be changed. Once someone establishes this type of trust, he cannot change the beneficiaries, he cannot alter the terms of the trust, and he cannot arbitrarily remove the trustee. Once you select the terms of this trust and sign the document, you have to walk away from it and let it do its job.

This is just one reason why it is critical to have an attorney and financial advisor who understand irrevocable life insurance trusts, because once the trust is established it cannot be changed. Again, a good place to find professionals who understand ILITs and how they can affect domestic partners through The National Institute for Domestic Partner Estate Planning. (www.NIDPestateplanning.com). Unlike a revocable living trust you and your partner can change at any time, it becomes extremely important for the ILIT to be done right the first time.

A few years ago, a couple came to me with their irrevocable life insurance trust, and they were practically in tears. Apparently, they read about an ILIT, examined the size of their estate, and then realized they needed one to avoid estate taxes on their $1 million life insurance policy. However, they had called several attorneys about drafting one for them, and they did not want to spend even the lowest price given of $1,000 to complete the trust paperwork. Instead, they found some forms somewhere and wrote it themselves.

In writing their own irrevocable life insurance trust, they named their oldest son as trustee and their younger son as the alternate trustee. They had also named both of their sons as the beneficiaries of the trust to split the proceeds equally. Being satisfied they had done everything correctly, they transferred their life insurance policy into the trust and rested easy believing everything was OK.

Unfortunately as the years passed, their two sons had a falling out and their families did not speak to each other. No matter how much the parents tried, the two brothers refused to reconcile. As sometimes happens in life, tragedy struck and the younger son died leaving a wife and two children behind. When the parents reviewed their estate plans including the irrevocable life insurance trust, they realized they had made no provisions if one of their sons died before them.

Now the couple was stuck with a permanent life insurance policy inside of an irrevocable trust that would only pay out to the older son and completely cut out the two grandchildren from the deceased son. When I explained there was nothing I or any other attorney could do to change the irrevocable trust for them and the best they could do is alter the rest of their estate to try to even things out, they grew more upset and simply left. What I did not have to say to them was this could have easily been avoided if an experienced attorney had drafted the trust for them in the first place. But I knew if they had foreseen the problems they now had, they would have gladly paid an attorney to draft the trust correctly.

You lose control over life insurance

In order for the proceeds of the life insurance policy to stay outside of your taxable estate when you pass on, you also have to give up all control over the life insurance policy. Once the policy is in the trust, you have to leave the management of the policy in the hands of your trustee.

I can imagine the people reading this are now ready to give up on using this kind of trust because they don't want the trustee to do whatever they want with the policy. There are some definite safeguards in place to make sure the trustee does not "steal" your life insurance proceeds. The trustee of an irrevocable life insurance trust is under a legal duty to administer the policy for the benefit of the beneficiaries of the trust. Therefore, the trustee cannot change the beneficiaries of the trust and must keep the trust as the beneficiary of the policy. The trustee is also under an obligation to use his or her best judgment to manage the trust for the sake of the beneficiaries and not themselves. There is no reason for you and your partner to be afraid of utilizing a properly drafted and executed irrevocable life insurance trust... as long as you chose the right trustee.

Another important factor to consider is the kind of life insurance you will use. These days, there are many different life insurance policies with plenty of "bells and whistles" to handle all kinds of needs. In many cases, certain life insurance policies can double as excellent tax-free or tax-deferred retirement accounts. Because of the special tax status many life insurance policies enjoy, there are many creative (and legal) ways to grow your assets while avoiding taxes. In most cases, these policies are not appropriate for an irrevocable life insurance trust because you can no longer reach those "retirement assets."

By far, term insurance is the most appropriate type of life insurance policy for an irrevocable life insurance trust. By term insurance, I mean the traditional means of paying a premium to be covered for a set amount over a period of time. For example, you pay an annual premium of $6,000 for 20 years to have $1 million of coverage in case you pass on. After 20 years if you have not passed on the policy is terminated, or in some cases it can be renewed, likely at a much higher premium.

The reason that term insurance is the most appropriate policy for an ILIT is giving up control of the policy not much of a sacrifice. There are no funds you need to access that you wouldn't have already paid to the insurance company. If you completely change your mind about the terms of the irrevocable life insurance trust, you can simply not give the premium to the trust and the policy (and then the trust) dies. At this point, you can completely start over with a new policy and new trust without losing anything of value, except you may have to pay a higher premium because of age or other factors.

Other policies may also be appropriate for an irrevocable life insurance trust, again provided you are willing to completely part company with the cash value in the policy. For example, there are some permanent life insurance policies that are nothing more than paid up life insurance good for the remainder of your life or until a very old age. The major advantage is you have the insurance permanently as opposed to a term policy that terminates after a set number of years, and at some point you no longer have to pay any premiums. The main characteristic of these kinds of policies that make them appropriate for an ILIT is they have no value you can access, and therefore giving control over to the trustee of an irrevocable trust does not affect your current cash flow.

A few years ago, I was working with a newer financial advisor to help a domestic partner couple plan their estates. One member of the couple was about 20 years older than the other and was the primary wage earner in the family. While the other member had some inherited assets, he was no longer earning any outside wages. In looking at the couple's financial situation, the advisor was eager and fairly knowledgeable, and he certainly knew enough to call me for advice. After describing their financial situation and determining it was likely there would be estate taxes if the life insurance proceeds were included in the either partners taxable estate, we began to discuss the possibility of using an ILIT. The advisor had some knowledge of what an irrevocable life insurance trust was and how it worked, but had not yet worked with a client on establishing one.

When we began discussing the type of life insurance policy he was recommending to the clients, it was quickly apparent the policy did not fit. On one hand, the older client wanted to use the life insurance policy as a type of tax deferred investment vehicle to borrow against (which can be done with the right policy). On the other hand, he also wanted to provide a lump sum of cash for his partner that would not be subject to estate taxes. Because any policy in the irrevocable life insurance trust must be out of the client's control, this type of policy was not going to work. Instead, we discussed the client's goals and recommended two policies; one as a permanent life insurance policy to be placed into the ILIT with the premiums paid over several years, and a second life insurance policy with a low death benefit but with an investment component that was tax-favorable.

An independent trustee is needed

Another important element in setting up an irrevocable life insurance trust is assigning an independent trustee to manage the trust. By independent, I do not necessarily mean hiring a corporate trust company, although this is certainly an option. I mean the trustee should be a person whom you and your partner trust who has some financial knowledge and is willing to work well with your financial advisor. The trustee cannot be your partner, nor should it be a child or parent of either of you. If the trustee is your partner, it is certain that the IRS would state that because your partner was the trustee and beneficiary of the trust, he had complete control over the assets and therefore all of the assets in the trust would be included in *this* taxable estate, which is precisely what we want to avoid by having the life insurance trust in the first place.

I also acknowledge I am breaking with the common legal thought and even some current determinations of the IRS by stating you should not name a child or parent as trustee, but the definition of an independent trustee means the person cannot be unduly influenced by the person setting up the trust by virtue of their relationship. Spouses are automatically rejected as not being independent, and I personally do not see too much difference in the closeness of relationship in the "immediate family." Therefore, out of an admitted abundance of caution, I recommend you have an adult sibling or other trusted family member or friend as the trustee of your irrevocable life insurance trust.

While the trustee must be independent, he also should be a person whom you and your partner trust to manage the funds properly and look out for the best interests of the beneficiaries. While your sister may be the most financially savvy person you know and you trust her and her abilities, if she has a bad relationship with your partner, she might not be looking out for your partner and would not make a good trustee. On the other hand, if your partner's brother is also financially astute and your partner trusts he will look out for your partner's best interests, it does not really matter if your relationship with him is a little cold. After all, the ILIT is not really for your benefit but is instead for the benefit of your partner.

Formalities must be observed

There are numerous legal elements that must be included within the language of your trust, but there is also a strict procedure that governs how life insurance premiums must be paid in order for the trust to work. *The biggest and most costly mistakes you can make are ignoring the technical formalities surrounding the trust after it has been put in place.* The basic steps for establishing and maintaining the trust are as follows:

Step One: Review insurance options with your financial advisor and determine what kind of policy would be best under the circumstances.

Step Two: Have a skilled estate planning attorney draft the irrevocable trust, and then you and the independent trustee sign the document.

Step Three: Give the initial premium payment to the trustee.

Step Four: The trustee must send a form letter to your partner (and possibly the contingent beneficiaries) stating the partner has received a "gift" and has a certain period of time to "claim" it.

Step Five: The partner, and any other beneficiaries, must send the form back stating they do not wish to claim the gift and it is therefore to be held by the trustee for their benefit (or alternatively the beneficiary simply does not respond within the time stated in the letter).

Step Six: The trustee applies for the life insurance policy with the trust as both the owner and the beneficiary and pays the premium.

Step Seven: Repeat steps three through five each time a payment is given to the trustee before the premium is paid to the insurance company.

Again, the formalities are important to establish you are giving up control of the trust and the beneficiaries are indeed given some time frame in which to claim their "gift" or leave it with the trustee. Because of the procedures involved, it is generally recommended the premiums be paid well ahead of time and the premiums be handled annually. You can imagine the paperwork and headaches involved if the trustee had to follow this procedure monthly, so making this process a once a year duty will be greatly appreciated by the trustee.

This is also a good time to discuss the legal rules versus the practical aspects of gifting to fund the life insurance trust. In order to preserve your estate tax credits and avoid potential gift taxes, the amount you are gifting to any one individual cannot exceed $12,000 per year. If the premiums on the life insurance policy exceed $12,000 annually, the trust should list more than just your partner as a beneficiary who will receive the funds

Three-year rule

Another formality that needs to be observed is purchasing the insurance through the irrevocable life insurance trust with the trustee applying for the policy. But this is in the best of all possible worlds. In some cases, you may not be able to get a new life insurance policy and may need to stay with the policy you already have. Some of these reasons include a much higher premium because of age, or straight out uninsurability because of health problems.

If you already have a life insurance policy and because of expense or uninsurability you wish to keep the existing policy, you can always transfer the policy into the irrevocable life insurance trust. If you do, you must be aware you must outlive the transfer of the policy into the trust by three years in order for the life insurance to be excluded from your taxable estate.

For example, if in 2011 George wants to leave everything to Lionel, but the value of his successful dry cleaning business plus life insurance means his estate will incur a large amount of estate taxes. Specifically, if George's business is worth $2 million and he has a life insurance policy with a $2 million benefit, he has a taxable estate of $4 million. A $4 million estate would equate to $1,365,000 in estate taxes. However, if his life insurance proceeds were taken out of the estate tax equation, the taxable estate would be $2 million, equaling $435,000 in estate taxes. That saved $930,000 in estate taxes.

If George has significant health problems and cannot get a new insurance policy, he has to stay with the existing policy and transfer it into an irrevocable life insurance trust with Lionel as the beneficiary. If George transfers the policy into an irrevocable life insurance trust on July 1, 2011, and passes on in August of 2014, George's life insurance is not part of his taxable estate. Using the $2 million business value, George's estate has to pay $435,000 in estate taxes. If George passes on in June of 2014, George's life insurance is part of his taxable estate, and the $2 million business and $2 million life insurance value leads to $1,365,000 in estate taxes.

While transferring a life insurance policy into an ILIT is not as ideal as applying for a life insurance policy through the trustee of the ILIT, it is often worth the expense of setting up the ILIT and transferring the policy into the trust unless there is a high probability the person will pass on in the next three years. In the end, there is a relatively small expense in potentially saving hundreds of thousands of dollars, whereas if nothing is done, it is certain the life insurance proceeds will trigger hundreds of thousands of dollars in estate taxes.

Multiple tax savings

In planning to avoid unnecessary estate taxes for my domestic partner clients, I often come across what I call the "one-step" tax savings mindset. Partners often indicate their primary concern is providing for each other, and estate tax planning may be a large part of that. After all, money paid to the federal government through taxes is not there for their partner to utilize.

However, an irrevocable life insurance trust can be set up so it can avoid estate taxes *twice*. An ILIT can be created so once the life insurance pays into the trust for the benefit of the partner, the trustee remains in control of the trust *including having sole discretion of whether or not to distribute funds to the partner.* If the appropriate language is included denying outright control over the funds to the partner, the life insurance would not be included in the partner's estate either.

For example, if in 2011 Kate and Allie are partners, Allie has a $2 million business and $2 million in life insurance, and Kate has $1 million in investments and their home, an irrevocable life insurance trust for Allie seems wholly appropriate.

Depending on the whether or not an irrevocable life insurance trust is used, and further depending on whether or not control of the assets inside the trust were ever given to Kate, there are several possible estate tax situations:

- If Allie did not use an irrevocable life insurance trust, her $4 million estate would pay $1,375,000 in estate taxes. Assuming no growth or depreciation, when Kate passes on with her $1 million and the $2,625,000 she inherited from Allie, her taxable estate would be $3,625,000, meaning Kate's estate would have to pay $1,198,750 in estate taxes. Under this scenario, a total of $2,573,750 would be paid in estate taxes from both estates, and only $2,426,250 of the original $5 million will be passed on to the next generation.

- If Allie did use an irrevocable life insurance trust, her estate would only be $2 million, leaving a tax bill of $435,000. Assuming no growth and no depreciation and assuming that Kate directly inherits the $2 million from Allie's ILIT, when Kate passes on with $1 million and the $3,565,000 she inherited from Allie, her estate would be $4,565,000, meaning Kate's estate would have to pay $1,640,550 in estate taxes. Under this scenario, a total of $2,075,550 would be paid in estate taxes from both estates, and only $2,924,450 of the original $5 million will be passed on to the next generation.

- If Allie did use an irrevocable life insurance trust, her estate would only be $2 million, leaving a tax bill of $435,000. Assuming no growth and no depreciation and assuming the $2 million in the ILIT is left in the control and discretion of the trustee so the trustee can give Kate money if she needs and requests it, when Kate passes on with $1 million and the $1,565,000 she inherited from Allie, her estate would be $2,565,000, meaning Kate's estate would have to pay $700,550 in estate taxes. Under this scenario, a total of $1,135,550 would be paid in estate taxes from both estates, and $3,864,450 of the original $5 million will be passed on to the next generation.

In the last scenario, having the irrevocable life insurance trust provide for the trustee to discretionarily provide for Kate rather than distribute the assets to Kate directly, the next generation will inherit an additional $940,000. That's almost an additional $1 million saved in estate taxes. As long as the right, "trusted" trustee is chosen who will legitimately use the trust funds for Kate's needs, it is definitely worth looking at using the ILIT for two transfers rather than one.

Summary

An irrevocable life insurance trust can certainly provide a lot of value in reducing or sometimes eliminating estate taxes. For domestic partners specifically, or even generally for all unmarried individuals, life insurance can tremendously increase a taxable estate, reducing the benefits you want to leave your partner. If you are willing to give up control of life insurance to a trustee, if you are willing to establish beneficiaries through the trust knowing they can never be changed, and if you are willing to follow the formalities in setting up and maintaining an irrevocable life insurance trust, an ILIT may significantly increase what you leave behind for your partner and to future generations.

Chapter Thirteen:
Using Corporations and
Other Business Entities

Some of the most complicated, yet successful, methods of reducing taxable estates for domestic partners are some pretty creative transactions involving corporations and other business entities. In this chapter, we will review a few of the concepts surrounding these transactions, provide a few examples, and give some strong words of caution. Because of the complexity of the techniques, we will not go too in depth. In fact, because each situation is different and requires individual counseling, I would recommend you speak with an experienced estate planning attorney about these techniques if you are even considering using some of them.

Two additional notes. First, we will only use the term "corporation" in this chapter, although there are a variety of other business entities with which these concepts work well. In fact, some business entities may work better than others, and this is yet an additional reason to talk to an estate planning attorney before jumping into these waters. (One such form is a Family Limited Partnership, but because of its complexity it will not be covered in this book. For a free copy of a report on just Family Limited Partnerships, please go to www.domesticpartnerflps.com and download the free report.) Second, these tactics only apply to business assets. Placing your personal residence or personal investments inside a corporate entity does not do anything to decrease estate taxes.

While there are additional concepts in the complex field of reducing the value of taxable estates, there are three main concepts or "discounts" on which we will focus:

1) minority interest discount

2) lack of marketability discount

3) lack of shareholder rights discount.

Before moving into the specifics, let's first discuss what discounts are. By "discount," I mean the value of corporate interests or shares is actually lower than the value of the assets they represent. Please bear with me because this is one of the most difficult concepts for even new attorneys and accountants to understand, because I am about to correctly tell you that 2+2=3.

Whenever someone owns corporate shares, he owns a part of a company. That company has assets, and those assets have value. The value of the shares, however, does not equal the value of the assets in the company. The value of the shares depend a great deal on other factors, not the least of which is how business professionals think the company will perform in the coming months and years.

For example, if a person possesses 1,000 shares of XYZ Corporation, and there are only 100,000 shares, then the person owns 1 percent of XYZ Corporation. If professionals looking at the market see how the company has performed over the last few years, take into account product and service lines, and a myriad of other factors, they may say the value of each share is $10. Intuitively, we can presume the 1 percent interest in the company is worth $10,000, and therefore the whole company must be worth $1,000,000.

The fact is the stock as a whole *may* be worth that much, but what about the assets inside XYZ Corporation? What someone would pay for the building the company owns as its headquarters, the machinery and supplies may very well be worth $1.5 million or only $500,000. What is critical to determining stock price is the company as a whole and how it performs. (Trust me —presume I am telling you the truth when I say the value of the corporate ownership shares are not the same as the value of the assets inside the company. If you don't believe me, then please put this book down and spend some time talking through this concept with an economics or business educator). What is important for estate tax purposes is the value of the corporate shares in small corporations, and taking into account the various discounts, is what is important, not the value of the assets inside the corporation.

Now, with those concepts in mind, imagine you want to reduce the value of your taxable estate, and one of your biggest assets is a piece of rental property on the beach. If the house is valued at $1 million, that is the amount included in your taxable estate. But if the house were owned by a corporation, run as a rental property business, and all of the other principles are applied in valuing the shares of stock and not the house, your combined shares may be valued at only $850,000.

Discounts

To further complicate things, the value of the shares of stock in a small, closely held corporation can be lowered even further depending on how the shares are owned and what power the shares may represent. The three additional "discounts' we will discuss are 1) minority interest discount 2) lack of marketability discount and 3) lack of shareholder rights discount. All of these discounts come about because each lowers what someone is willing to pay for the shares of stock if offered.

Minority interest discount

There is a discount available when a person does not own enough shares to control the direction of the company. Typically, this level is when a person has 50 percent or less in corporation ownership. The reason for this discount is that a person would pay less for shares of stock when he is not able to control the direction of the corporation, and therefore determine his own fate. He is instead left at the mercy of others who will hopefully increase the value of the shares and pay out dividends.

Using a simple example to illustrate this concept in reverse, assume Investor A owns 45 percent of XYZ Corporation, Investor B owns 49 percent, and Investor C owns 6 percent. Under this situation, if you were buying into the company you may only pay $10 per share for all of the shares from any one of these Investors. After all, even if you purchased all of Investor B's shares and owned 49 percent of the company, you would still have to convince one of the other investors to change the course of the company.

Now imagine you do own the 49 percent, and Investor C was willing to sell her shares to you or Investor A. Now what are the shares worth? Substantially more since whoever purchased them would be able to effectively control the direction of the company without having to convince anyone else. Perhaps even $20 a share is not unreasonable if it meant control of the company.

The original $10 per share represents the value of the shares with a minority interest discount. In other words, someone is willing to pay less just because he would not have control over the company. If you owned the shares at $10 a share and not $20 per share when you passed on, then, obviously, the amount of value in your taxable estate is less, and therefore there are fewer taxes to pay.

Lack of marketability discount

There is also a discount available if someone was not able to sell her shares to just anyone on the open market, meaning there was a "lack of marketability." While this is not typical in large corporations, and certainly not publicly held corporations where the stock is available for purchase on the open market, it is very common in small businesses.

Typically, small businesses owned by more than one person are only owned by a handful of people who only want to work with each other. Therefore, it is typical for small corporations to have a document called a shareholder agreement preventing the owners from selling their shares to anyone outside of the existing owners without going through a substantial process, including offering the shares for the same price to the existing owners. After all, three people who own a construction company don't want two of them to walk into work on a Monday morning and find out they have a new partner because the third person sold his shares.

By having a shareholder agreement in place, the company has protected itself from having surprise owners showing up. While this may be a good thing for the company, not being able to sell shares to whomever one wants also means the fair market value of the shares is substantially less. If you were just an investor, why would you want to buy shares of stock in a company you could not simply sell and get out of any time you wished? You may invest, but you would only be willing to pay less.

Again, because the value of your shares under these conditions is less than if you were able to sell to anyone, the value of the shares in your taxable estate is also less. If you and your partner owned all of the shares in a candy store and executed a shareholder's agreement stating you could not sell to anyone outside of your partner, the value of the shares would also be considerably less.

Lack of shareholder rights discount

We have already discussed minority interest discounts and lack of marketability discounts, and they are technically "lack of shareholder rights" discounts. But we are talking about something a little different. A lack of shareholder rights really means a person's shares in the company do not entitle him to vote at all, do not entitle him to regular dividends, and do not entitle him to voice his opinion at meetings.

By denying these rights for certain classes of shares, the value of the shares are further discounted. At this point, you may be asking, why would anyone want to buy shares in a corporation if they were under all of these restrictions? That's the point. The value of the shares is significantly less, and therefore the value of the shares when computed as part of a taxable estate is also significantly less. However, the shares also represent a company that has assets worth value.

To receive a free gift worth $39.97, please go to
www.estateplanningfordomesticpartners.com/gift

Now, for the big tie-in with the next chapter — these discounts mean one partner can gift more of her assets to the other in order to equalize their estates using these corporate discounts. This is in addition to how the discounts may also lower their taxable estate if they passed on.

Let's use an example combining all three of these discounts. Suppose a corporation has both controlling shares, called common stock, and limited shares that were not marketable. Nor could the owner of them vote or demand dividends. The corporation owned a shopping mall that kept increasing in value each year. However, the owners of the limited shares did not receive many dividends.

On the surface, and in properly valuing the shares of the corporation, let's say that a person holding 25 percent of the limited shares has them valued at $250,000. In reality, let's assume that the corporation has all of the shares of common stock owned by a father, and the four children own all of the limited shares equally.

When the father passes on, only the value of the shares at $2 million is counted and not the value of the whole mall, which is $4 million. Now the children would receive 25 percent of the common stock shares each to match their limited shares. They then close the company and sell the mall. Each of them would have started with $250,000 ($1 million total among the four children) and end up with $1 million each, and the father's estate would have been taxed at $2 million in shares of stock, not the $4 million total. If you do the math, there is an extra $1 million that was not present before, and therefore was not subject to any estate taxes. Depending on the other assets in the father's estate, that could have resulted in nearly $500,000 in taxes saved.

Words of caution

I know I mentioned it before, but to take full advantage of these corporate techniques without mistakes, it is important to work through qualified professionals to properly establish and maintain your businesses, and therefore potential estate tax savings. There are four specific things I would like to warn you about:

- This only works for business assets.

- An attorney is needed to establish the businesses.

- A CPA is needed to evaluate the business.

- There are ongoing formalities needed.

- These business entities must work with your trust.

Business assets

Time and again, I have heard of people conducting seminars about how they can devalue their estate and provide asset protection by putting everything they own into a corporation or, more commonly, a family limited partnership. They'll collect a hefty fee for the paperwork, and tell the seminar attendee to put everything into the business. This does not work.

The fact is if the IRS took a look at the "business," they would not give any discounts because the corporation was not involved in business. If the person was sued and a court looked at the business, they would find there was no corporate protection. Unless you and your partner are engaging in business with the assets you want to discount, such as rental property, this technique will not work.

Attorney assistance

It is also imperative you use an attorney to help you choose the right business entity and set it up properly. Because there are a multitude of different kinds of businesses you can use and some are more appropriate than others, be sure to get assistance in choosing the one that is right for you and your partner.

An attorney is also critical to making sure all of the correct steps are taken. I often come across do-it-yourself clients who took the first step of filing the correct paperwork with the North Carolina Secretary of State, and then ignored all of the other legal paperwork needed for years. Had I set the company up for them, I would have created corporate bylaws, held annual meetings, and made sure the annual paperwork was filed with the Secretary of State's office. When I mention this paperwork to the do-it-yourselfers, I usually get a shrug and "well, how was I supposed to know?"

Unfortunately, not knowing about the paperwork does not mean the IRS will let you get away with the discounts.

CPA assistance

Another important factor, and unfortunately an additional expense, is to have a CPA involved in valuing the business. As we will discuss in the next chapter, domestic partners with unequal assets who want to equalize them may want to transfer as much property as they can from one partner to the other. One way to transfer more each year without incurring gift taxes is to gift corporate shares (or sell them) to your partner. Because they are discounted, you can transfer more each year. However, to sell or gift shares at a discounted price, the shares have to be evaluated each year this is done.

In addition to having the shares valued and the paperwork filed properly, there may be business tax returns requiring the help of a CPA. The fact is if you and your partner have enough assets such that you are considering using business entities to reduce potential estate taxes, you probably need the help of a CPA in doing your tax returns anyway. At this level, if you are doing your own taxes, you are probably missing out on a lot of deductions. I have personally found a good CPA is more than worth their fees in finding deductions.

Ongoing formalities

All corporations and business entities need some ongoing care. Legally, corporations are separate entities, and certain things need to happen at least on an annual basis. For instance, all corporations need to have annual shareholder and board of director meetings, and minutes of these meetings should be taken. Even the clients I work with who are a sole shareholder, director and the only officer need to have minutes of their annual meetings taken, signed and placed in their corporate record book.

Another important formality is to make sure each business entity has its own taxpayer ID number and bank account. All business revenue and expenses should be run through the business, and all personal expenses should not. Paying personal expenses with a business check or paying business expenses with personal checks not only confuses your accountant, but may also leave your personal assets open to business lawsuits. Again, the importance of having an attorney and accountant work with you and your partner can not be overstated.

Working With Your Trust

While using corporations or other business entities can help reduce your taxable estate, corporate shares are assets that would go through probate if they were in your name. In order to avoid this, you and your partner need to make sure all business shares are owned in the name of your revocable living trust. Further, both partners need to make sure they are accounting for their own ownership interests in the businesses through the domestic partnership property agreement.

As with any other coordinated plan, there may be independent working parts, but they are all tied together. Using corporations or other business entities as part of your life and estate plan may make sense for you and your partner, but be sure to have these entities work with your revocable living trust.

Summary

High estate values equates into high estate taxes. Depending on the estate values of domestic partners, utilizing corporations or other business entities may make sense. However, care should be taken to use the right professionals to help you, observing the formalities, and making sure that the entities work with your revocable living trust.

Chapter Fourteen:
Estate Equalization Planning

As with all things in life, not everything is as equal as we may want. Domestic partners find each other and make a commitment, and the value of their estates is an afterthought. But once they make that commitment, there may be a desire to shift assets from one partner to the other to "even things out."

Aside from a feeling of equalization, partners may also have sound estate and income tax planning reasons to even things out. If one partner has the bulk of the couple's assets and is the "breadwinner" of the family, investments and work income may push that partner's income taxes into the stratosphere while the other partner may not be earning any income from her efforts or investments. In addition, a quick estate tax analysis may show some severe tax ramifications if the partner with the bulk of the assets passed on second.

But, keeping in mind gift tax consequences, how far can $12,000 a year go? The answer is, over time, it can go a long way. That is why it is strongly recommended that lower current value, high growth and high income potential assets be transferred first so that it can grow in the partner's estate.

Example

Let's assume Jeff owns an online news company, and Karl is his stay-at-home partner. Jeff also inherited a few million dollars in real estate and investments from his uncle Richard, and the investments also bring in a substantial amount of money each year. If Jeff has a $3 million potential estate, and Karl has a $50,000 potential estate, even having a Partner AB-SECURE™ Trust would have little estate tax savings if Karl passed on first. Taking a look at both situations for potential estate taxes:

- *Karl passes on first in 2011, then Jeff six months later:* Karl leaves his $50,000 to the SECURE™ Trust, protecting it from future estate taxes. Jeff passes on six months later, leaving $3 million to his and Karl's nephew Rick, along with a tax bill of $905,000, and the $50,000 from the SECURE™ Trust. The total net estate to Rick is $2,145,000.

- *Jeff passes on first in 2011, then Karl six months later:* Jeff passes on leaving $1 million to the SECURE™ Trust, protecting it from future estate taxes, and leaving the rest to Karl through the B Trust. Karl passes on six months later, leaving $2,050,000 to Rick, along with a tax bill of $458,500, and the $1 million from the SECURE™ Trust. The total net estate to Rick is $2,591,500.

Depending on who passes on first, there can be a difference of $446,500 in federal estate taxes. This "extra" tax would have been eliminated if Karl had $1 million to fully fund the SECURE™ Trust. Now, I'm not saying that Jeff *has* to transfer $1 million of his assets over time to Karl. That decision is up to Jeff and Karl. But Jeff and Karl should also know what the tax ramifications are if they do nothing.

Choosing assets

Assuming Jeff and Karl want to equalize their assets more, they are limited by the $12,000 per year without incurring gift taxes. With this in mind, choosing the right assets to transfer each year is critical. Because transferring the right assets is so important, Jeff and Karl would probably use the assistance of their financial advisor to choose them. The following are assets the financial advisor would likely recommend examining for possible transfer:

- Small business stock or interests while the business is fairly stable but still growing.

- Interests in rental property, or corporate interests that hold rental property.

- Interests in the primary or other residences likely to appreciate significantly with time.

- Stock in established companies that may not have a high value but pay out good dividends (such as the limited rights shares discussed in the last chapter).

The idea is to transfer assets at a discounted value early so they can grow substantially while possessed by the receiving partner, and not while in the hands of the giving partner. One of the reasons for discounting corporate assets as discussed in the previous chapter is to get more assets to the partner more quickly.

If $12,000 of limited partner interests in a family limited partnership will pay out $2,000 a year in dividends but have no growth in value, getting those interests from Jeff to Karl would still be $12,000 of limited partnership interests in 20 years, but it would also pay out $40,000 to Karl over those 20 years. If the funds were put into an account that paid 7 percent interest compounded annually, this one gift of $12,000 in limited partnership interests would total $87,224.04 plus the $12,000 in limited shares.

And this is just from one transfer of $12,000 worth of limited interests. If the same limited partnership interest was transferred each year from Jeff to Karl also paying out the same $2,000 a year but not growing in value, over 20 years Jeff would have transferred $723,993.17 in income and $240,000 in limited partnership interests. Over 20 years, this gift of just $12,000 each year transferred nearly $1 million to Karl from Jeff.

Transferring assets each year

Of course, you may not want to transfer the same kind of asset each year, depending on how certain assets are performing. If a real estate investment is about to take off, Jeff may want to transfer some of those interests to Karl. If it is expected some of the limited partnership interests are not going to pay dividends at all over the next few years, Jeff may want to gift some of his traditional, publicly traded stock to Karl for a few years.

The point is each annual gift from one partner to another should reflect an informed decision based on current projections after discussing things with your financial advisor. Gifting the same type of asset each year may not necessarily hurt things, but it could result in lower than possible growth in the estate of the receiving partner.

Another consideration is at some point, the estates may have equalized but continue to grow in the receiving partner's possession. If because of proper planning Jeff and Karl now have $2 million in assets each but all of the growing assets are in Karl's name, there may now be a growing discrepancy in their assets. But this time, Karl's assets are greater than Jeff's!

In this instance, and possibly even before it gets to this point, Jeff and Karl can always *exchange* assets. In other words, Jeff and Karl can begin trading assets between each other in order to properly balance not only the value but also the growth and income of their assets. However, this should not be done without the assistance of a CPA to properly document the exchanges (and avoid them being counted as "gifts").

Summary

While there is a low threshold for giving gifts from one partner to the other, there is considerable room to equalize the value in each partner's possession. By choosing the right assets over time, and by working in combination with the principles of discounting of business shares discussed in the previous chapter, domestic partners can equalize their estates within a Partner AB-SECURE™ Trust and minimize estate taxes.

Made in the USA
Charleston, SC
18 May 2012